The Orchestra: A Very Short Introduction

VERY SHORT INTRODUCTIONS are for anyone wanting a stimulating and accessible way in to a new subject. They are written by experts and have been published in more than 25 languages worldwide.

The series began in 1995 and now represents a wide variety of topics in history, philosophy, religion, science, and the humanities. The VSI library now contains more than 300 volumes—a Very Short Introduction to everything from ancient Egypt and Indian philosophy to conceptual art and cosmology—and will continue to grow in a variety of disciplines.

Very Short Introductions available now:

For more information visit our web site

www.oup.co.uk/general/vsi/

D. Kern Holoman

THE
ORCHESTRA

A Very Short Introduction

OXFORD
UNIVERSITY PRESS

OXFORD
UNIVERSITY PRESS

Oxford University Press is a department of the University of Oxford.
It furthers the University's objective of excellence in research,
scholarship, and education by publishing worldwide.

Oxford   New York
Auckland   Cape Town   Dar es Salaam   Hong Kong   Karachi
Kuala Lumpur   Madrid   Melbourne   Mexico City   Nairobi
New Delhi   Shanghai   Taipei   Toronto

With offices in
Argentina   Austria   Brazil   Chile   Czech Republic   France   Greece
Guatemala   Hungary   Italy   Japan   Poland   Portugal   Singapore
South Korea   Switzerland   Thailand   Turkey   Ukraine   Vietnam

Oxford is a registered trade mark of Oxford University Press
in the UK and certain other countries.

Published in the United States of America by
Oxford University Press
198 Madison Avenue, New York, NY 10016

Library of Congress Cataloging-in-Publication Data
Holoman, D. Kern, 1947–
The orchestra : a very short introduction / D. Kern Holoman.
p.   cm.
Includes bibliographical references and index.
ISBN 978-0-19-976028-2 (pbk. : alk. paper)
1. Orchestra—History. I. Title.
ML1200.H65   2012
784.2—dc23   2011053216

Printed by Integrated Books International, United States of America
on acid-free paper

Contents

List of illustrations

Chapter 1
Philharmonia

The philharmonic society, a local coalition of players, listeners, and financial backers, was established to sponsor public concerts of orchestral music. In due course it owned buildings and inventory. From the very first it was a locus of civic pride, holding much in common with the other institutions that anchor urban systems—hospitals, libraries, playhouses, zoos, public gardens.

In the early philharmonic society the identity of the orchestral players was of less consequence than the sponsoring of the concerts. Musicians were engaged from existing theater and court orchestras, a simple enough transaction during Lent (and in some places Advent), when the theaters were closed. Their stipends represented a welcome, if token, addition to their primary income. A philharmonic's defining mission was, and remains, to present orchestra concerts in a dedicated space, on consideration of a paid ticket. Concerts came in series, or seasons, perhaps six or eight at a stretch. Subscribers were impressively loyal, buying out the better seasons year after year and passing their right to subscribe on to their heirs.

"Going to Symphony was the summit of the musical experience," writes Alan Rich of the half century, roughly 1930 to 1980, when the symphony orchestra dominated the menu of leisure interests. More even than opera, seen as an extravagant, somewhat trivial plaything of the oligarchs, the philharmonic society crowned its culture. It was dignified, elevated in purpose, prone to stimulate the intellect. The orchestra hall came to be a recognized locus of the elegant things in life: going to symphony embraced fashionable clothing, fine dining, at length the purchase of records and record players. It was endlessly inviting, and cheap at the price.

The symphony orchestra had grown from that of Beethoven's time—a dozen in each string section, with pairs of woodwinds and brass and a percussionist or two—into the industrial-strength aggregation of today's philharmonic of 110 or more. The outward look of the institution became fixed, standardized, its equipment proudly symbolizing the furthest advance of the Age of Industry, its costume that of Queen Victoria and Prince Albert.

Such a perception masks the lightning-paced modernity of the twenty-first-century philharmonic, where the critical issues facing classical music play out every week. The questions are as old as the institution itself: how and even whether to advance the repertoire, how to enable artist musicians to achieve the social equality their gifts and long investment demand, how to weather competition from within and without. How, for that matter, to adapt to sea change in the world order. Who's listening, and why?

In September 2009, at the start of the symphony season in Detroit, the conductor Leonard Slatkin proposed having his orchestra play with its back to the audience ("Listeners are distracted by seeing the faces of the musicians; [they] will tire of looking at backsides and focus purely on the music"), cutting Rachmaninov's Second Symphony to twelve minutes, beginning Beethoven's Fifth in bar 6, after a motto opening so familiar as to have become, Slatkin says, banal. That same year saw the emergence of a YouTube Symphony Orchestra, auditioned by videos posted on a server, voted on by the "YouTube community," and brought to Carnegie Hall for a concert conducted by Michael Tilson Thomas on May 20, 2009. The concluding work, commissioned for the next San Francisco

Symphony season, was *Warehouse Medicine* by Mason Bates, a
disc jockey purveyor of "electronica" with a PhD in composition,
who controlled a rack of electronics in the percussion section
and wore a T-shirt. (Bates went on to be 2010–12 composer-in-
residence with the Chicago Symphony.) Slatkin's challenge seemed
wacky, while the YouTube venture seemed inevitable. Yet both
moments provoked response as to what is meaningful in art
music . . . which is what philharmonia was about to begin with.

Emergence of the symphony orchestra

The band that accompanied Monteverdi's opera *Orfeo* of 1607 was
symphonic in complexity if not in size: two groups of five strings,
some brass players (trombones, trumpets, wooden cornetts), a
pair of recorders, and a wagonload of underpinning keyboard
instruments, harps, and lutes. The opulent court orchestra for
Louis XIV at Versailles was the 24 Violons du Roi, the *grande
bande*, with six violins for the uppermost part, four violas each
for three middle parts, and six bass instruments—source of our
concept of string sections in the dozens and half-dozens. (Flutes,
oboes, and trumpets-and-drums were summoned as needed, along
with the keyboards.) Jean-Baptiste Lully, arriving at court in 1652,
demanded and was granted a smaller and more polished group,
the Petits Violons.

The *collegium musicum* exercises—"amicable musical get-
togethers"—in the Leipzig of Telemann and J. S. Bach drew
fifty or sixty musicians, students and professionals alike, twice
a week to a coffeehouse. Here it appears that in addition to the
ubiquitous cantatas for soloists, chorus, and orchestra in vogue
at the time, the substance of Bach's orchestral music was featured
as well. By the end of Bach's life it was the series of orchestra
concerts that mattered to an enthusiastic public, stimulating
the organization of a Grosse Concert-Gesellschaft, where the
sponsors were local merchants and the venue was a tavern, the
Three Swans.

The conservatory movement in Italy—conservators of children, i. e., orphanages—had since the late 1500s been generating musicians in sufficient number to establish a veritable ecosystem of well-trained players (and singers and composers). The pioneering English music historian Charles Burney describes the merry cacophony of one of the Naples conservatories in 1770, where

> On the first flight of stairs was a trumpeter, screaming upon his instrument till he was ready to burst; on the second was a french-horn, bellowing in the same manner. In the common practising room there was a *Dutch concert* [blab school, or better, free for all], consisting of seven or eight harpsichords, more than as many violins, and several voices, all performing differing things and in different keys.

Vivaldi's orchestra of young women orphans from the Ospedale della Pietà in Venice, where he was appointed *maestro di concerti* in 1716, was not dissimilar in structure and capability from Lully's in France—but for the obvious attractions of gender and age: "I vow to you," wrote the French tourist Charles de Brosses, "that there is nothing so diverting as the sight of a young and pretty nun in white habit, with a bunch of pomegranate blossoms over her ear, conducting the orchestra and beating time with all the grace and precision imaginable." Here Vivaldi's staggeringly large repertoire for orchestra, and chorus-with-orchestra, was born—in a church on Sundays and holidays, the "finest music" before "a vast audience": "'Tis the rendezvous of all the coquettes of Venice, and such as are fond of intrigues have here both their hands and hearts full."

In pre-Revolutionary Paris, a Lenten series called the *concert spirituel*, founded in 1725, was presented in the Tuileries Palace to ticketed subscribers. Listeners and the newspaper journalists took sides in sometimes noisy battles of taste; Dr. Burney reported that a certain M. Pagin, best pupil of the violinist Tartini, "had the *honour* of being hissed at the Concert Spirituel for daring to play in the Italian style, and this was the reason of his quitting the profession." Behind the scenes the profit motive, expressed in the buying and selling of the monopoly for public concerts, drove artistic decisions. The original series came to an end when the royal family was confined in the Tuileries Palace after 1789, by which juncture the transition from sacred music for chorus-and-orchestra to a secular orchestral repertoire was done: Haydn's six "Paris" symphonies, Nos. 82–87, were hungrily consumed at the Tuilieries and offshoot series like those of the Masonic Lodge (Concert de la Loge Olympique), where in 1785 Marie Antoinette attended the premiere of the Haydn symphony subsequently called La Reine.

Most concert music continued to take place in the princely salons. Haydn administered eighteen or so orchestral players retained by the Hungarian prince Nikolaus Esterházy for his pleasure, seeing to it that the musicians conducted themselves "soberly, modestly, quietly and honestly," appearing "neatly, in white stockings, white linen, powdered, with either pigtail or hair-bag." They provided music at mealtimes, sacred music, theater music, and orchestra concerts—the 1772 premiere, for instance, of Haydn's "Farewell" Symphony No. 45 in F♯ Minor, with its closing *coup de théâtre* reminding Prince Nikolaus that the players needed to go home to their wives and children. From the court orchestra established in Mannheim in 1720, usually described as "the best in Europe," Mozart and others absorbed much of a modern style that included clarinets and crescendos. "Its forte is thunder, its crescendo a cataract, its diminuendo a crystal-clear stream babbling away into the distance, its piano a breath of spring." It numbered just under fifty players.

Haydn's concerts in London in 1791–92 and 1794–95, for which his last dozen symphonies were composed and first performed, attest to the increasingly successful marriage of commerce and art. These were presented by Johann Peter

Salomon, a businessman, impresario, and front-desk violinist. "I am Salomon from London, and I have come to take you there," he told Haydn in Vienna: "tomorrow we shall conclude an agreement." Salomon sought to accommodate the rage for music sweeping English society. Haydn's personal presence in London incited "such a degree of enthusiasm in the audience as almost amounts to frenzy!"; a wag journalist noted how "Folks of Fashion eager seek / Sixteen Concerts in a Week." Seasons were fully sold, and the mechanisms for institutionalizing them began to fall into place.

Similar success was found by Mozart and then Beethoven in their one-composer "academy" concerts in Vienna. Many of these were presented at the Imperial Court Theater, the Burgtheater, erected alongside the imperial palace by Empress Maria Theresa in 1741. Here, after his move to Vienna, Mozart presented his work annually: in 1784 a program of three symphonies, a piano concerto, a piano fantasy, and an aria with orchestra. Here, too, Haydn was borne by sedan-chair into the first public performance of *The Creation*, March 19, 1799. Beethoven's Akademie of December 22, 1808, in the Theater an der Wien offered a program over four hours, where the Fifth and Sixth Symphonies were premiered, the Fourth Piano Concerto, and for a finale, the Choral Fantasy with Beethoven himself at the piano.

First philharmonics

Arguably the first to offer continuous seasons of multiple concerts was the Philharmonic Society of London, established in January 1813—by the same J. P. Salomon who had brought Haydn to England, along with the pianist Muzio Clementi and like-minded associates. At one hundred years of age, in 1912, it became the Royal Philharmonic Society. The first concert included symphonies of Haydn and Beethoven, and soon the promoters were routinely inviting foreigners to conduct a resident orchestra in their 800-seat venue in the Hanover Square Rooms. The annual season of eight concerts was popular enough to cause traffic jams: "It is requested," said the printed flyers, "that the Coachmen may be directed to *set down* and *take up* with their horses' heads towards Piccadilly." Among those who visited were the pioneers of conducting, Spohr and Berlioz; Wagner came, as did Dvořák and Tchaikovsky.

A philharmonic society of similar ambition was active in tsarist St. Petersburg as early as 1802, with the stated goals of stimulating interest in new music and of supporting widows and orphans of musicians. Its first production was Haydn's *The Creation;* its most interesting was the first performance, ever, of Beethoven's *Missa solemnis,* in April 1824. ("Your genius is centuries before its time," the society's representative wrote back to Beethoven.) By the fall of the Romanov dynasty in 1917, the organization had presented more than 200 concerts and was the principal occupant of a fine hall.

When the Three Swans concerts in Leipzig became too rowdy, the town council authorized remodeling of the guildhall of the cloth merchants, the Gewandhaus, for concert giving, thus meeting a central criterion of philharmonia—that it be the result of citizen initiative and the work of local businessmen. Leipzig was the perfect environment for a philharmonic orchestra. It was home to the music publishing house of Breitkopf & Härtel, founded in 1719. There was good reporting and critique in the *Allgemeine musikalische Zeitung* and subsequently in Schumann's newspaper, the *Neue Zeitschrift für Musik.* There were convenient rail connections early on. Mendelssohn took over the Gewandhaus Orchestra in 1835 and made it the best in Germany; in spring 1843 a new Leipzig Conservatory opened in the courtyard of the Gewandhaus. Concertgoers passed beneath a remark of Seneca chiseled into the lintel: *Res severa est verum gaudium:* True pleasure is serious business.

In Paris some eighty affiliates of the Conservatoire, much of the faculty and their best students, banded together to make an orchestra and offer public concerts, largely, at first, to investigate the symphonies of Beethoven. (It was the oboist Gustave Vogt, a military bandsman to Napoleon, who had brought back the description of Beethoven as "an unlicked bear.") The Société des Concerts was a democratic collective, choosing its conductor and officers by ballot. It is a significant distinction that the Société des Concerts belonged exclusively to the players, who were members for life. The Paris Conservatory Orchestra enjoyed many decades of full houses, sold out in full-season subscriptions.

When the Vienna Philharmonic Orchestra was established in 1842, the administration took its cue from the Paris constitution: members of the orchestra ran the organization and elected their conductor. In this case the membership was pre-formed, since members of the Vienna Opera orchestra simply became the Vienna Philharmonic during concert season. Vienna had enjoyed the enlightened activities of its Gesellschaft der Musikfreunde

1. The Paris Conservatory Orchestra in its Salle des Concerts, April 1843. Habeneck conducts with a violin bow, and the chorus is placed in front of the orchestra.

(Friends of Music, or Musikverein) since 1812, successor to a
Society of Aristocratic Ladies for the Promotion of the Good
and Useful. Among the founders of the Musikverein were the
court composer Antonio Salieri, a banker's wife and Jewish
bluestocking named Fanny von Arnstein, the leading Austrian
intellectuals, and the remarkable conductor Ignaz Franz von
Mosel. In short order they established a concert series, the Vienna
Conservatory, an oratorio society now known as the Vienna
Philharmonic Chorus, a library, and in 1870 the celebrated
concert hall that bears their name: the Musikverein. It did not
hurt that Archduke Rudolf, brother of the emperor and a student
of Beethoven, was a patron.

In the same year, 1842, the first American philharmonic society
was established in New York, offering a season of ten concerts to
139 subscribers by an orchestra of fifty-eight. Each of the players
made $25 for the season, at the end of which there was a small
surplus and a library of fifteen overtures, eight symphonies, and
three miscellaneous works. In its first hundred years the New
York Philharmonic canceled a single concert, on learning of the
assassination of Abraham Lincoln in 1865.

The Berlin Philharmonic followed in 1882, organized from a
privately owned orchestra into a collective with generous civic
subvention and a partnering agent-producer. The Berliners
continue to elect their musicians and conductor, with auditions
played before the entire membership. In 1999, for instance, the
English conductor Simon Rattle was elected to the Philharmonic
by 129 members in a secret process that seems much the same as a
papal consistory.

The Boston Symphony Orchestra, founded in 1881, was by sharp
contrast largely the work of one man, Henry L. Higginson.
Higginson had served in the Union army during the Civil War, then
made his money in the family brokerage business. His manifesto for
a new orchestra in Boston offered a quality product at low price to a

Orchestras by date of founding

Date	Orchestra	Venue
1781	Leipzig Gewandhaus Orchestra	(Third) Gewandhaus (1981)
1808	Frankfurt Museumsgesellschaft concerts	Alte Opera (Old Opera House; 1880)
1813	Royal Philharmonic Society, London	Funds projects but no longer occupies a concert venue
1815	Handel and Haydn Society, Boston	Symphony Hall (1900) and other historic Boston venues
1828	Société des Concerts du Conservatoire, Paris (now Orchestre de Paris)	Salle Pleyel (1927); scheduled to occupy Philharmonie de Paris, Parc de la Villette (2014)
1842	New York Philharmonic	Avery Fisher Hall, Lincoln Center for the Performing Arts (1962)
1842	Vienna Philharmonic Orchestra	Grosser Musikvereinssaal (1870)
1880	St. Louis Symphony Orchestra	Powell Hall (1925)
1881	Boston Symphony Orchestra	Symphony Hall (1900)
1882	Berlin Philharmonic Orchestra	Berliner Philharmonie (1963)

Date	Orchestra	Venue
1882	St. Petersburg Philharmonic Orchestra	Great Hall (Bolshoi Zal) of the Philharmonic Society (1839)
1888	Royal Concertgebouw Orchestra, Amsterdam	Concertgebouw (1888)
1891	Chicago Symphony Orchestra	Orchestra Hall (1904)
1900	Philadelphia Orchestra	Verizon Hall, Kimmel Center (2001)
1904	London Symphony Orchestra	Barbican Centre, London (1982)
1911	San Francisco Symphony	Louise M. Davies Symphony Hall (1980)
1918	Cleveland Orchestra	Severance Hall (1931)
1919	Los Angeles Philharmonic Orchestra	Walt Disney Concert Hall (2003)
1926	NHK Symphony Orchestra, Tokyo	NHK Hall (1972)
1930	BBC Symphony Orchestra	Barbican Centre, London (1982)
1936	Israel Philharmonic Orchestra (originally Palestine Orchestra)	Mann Auditorium (1957), Tel Aviv

Date	Orchestra	Venue
1937	NBC Symphony Orchestra (disbanded 1954)	NBC Studio 8-H, Rockefeller Center, New York (1933)
1959	Academy of St. Martin-in-the-Fields	Church of St. Martin-in-the-Fields, Trafalgar Square, London (1724)
1987	New World Symphony	SunTrust Pavilion, New World Center, Miami Beach (2011)
1999	West-Eastern Divan	touring venues; based in Seville, Spain
2009	YouTube Symphony Orchestra	Carnegie Hall (2009), Sydney Opera House (2011)

large public, the whole tightly controlled by him personally in order to guarantee that his organization would be competitive with "the great German orchestras." He did all the hiring and firing, and made up the deficits—leaving him free to indulge his whims and cater to his distaste for modern music and "the extreme modern style of conducting." He was so blind an admirer of all things German as to lead the BSO, with its proud Prussian-degreed conductor Karl Muck and thirty-eight German musicians, into a crisis of loyalties during World War I, and so bitter an opponent to organized labor that the BSO was the last major orchestra to unionize. (French players were soon in the ascendant, as well as three French conductors—Pierre Monteux, Henri Rabaud, and Charles

Munch—and, phenomenally, the Russian Serge Koussevitzky, who had come to Boston from Paris.) Higginson's guiding principle, however, was benevolent: for him it was a matter of faith than the orchestra was a path to civic and personal betterment.

Philharmonia and the Belle Époque

The 1880s and '90s were to the symphony orchestra what the 1780s and '90s had been to the Classical Style: a time of ongoing opportunity, unquenchable demand, and inexhaustible wealth. It is the period of the third and fourth symphonies of Brahms, Mahler's first four symphonies, the Franck Symphonic Variations and D-Minor Symphony, the "Enigma" Variations of Edward Elgar. Conductors, soloists, and full orchestras embarked on historic concert tours; Tchaikovsky came to New York to conduct during the inaugural concert at Carnegie Hall. Cities beyond the traditional musical capitals invested in modern orchestras and venues. The National Symphony Orchestra of Mexico traces its foundation to 1881; a Lima Philharmonic Society of 1907 was promoting orchestra concerts soon after. The year 1900 saw the establishment of the Philadelphia Orchestra and the opening of Symphony Hall in Boston.

The key figure in colonizing America with symphony orchestras was Theodore Thomas, who established the Chicago Symphony in 1891 and led it until his death in 1905. Emigrating from Germany with his parents, he joined the U.S. Navy band at the age of thirteen and the New York Philharmonic before he was twenty. He mastered the profession of conducting with orchestras accompanying European virtuosi on their coast-to-coast tours, notably those of Liszt's rival Sigismond Thalberg, and on the strength of that experience founded the Theodore Thomas Orchestra (1862). The Thomas Orchestra toured widely as well, establishing series in Philadelphia, St. Louis, Cincinnati, and Milwaukee from its home base in New York. It arrived for its first series in Chicago the day after the Great Fire in October 1871. Thomas went on to conduct the concerts of both the New York Philharmonic Society and the Brooklyn Philharmonic Society as well as the May Festival in Cincinnati, where he served briefly as director of the College Conservatory of Music. He was wooed to Chicago in 1889 by representatives of the city's business interests.

In the United States the period between the end of World War I and the Great Depression was fertile, the musical landscape enriched by the Cleveland, Detroit, and Los Angeles orchestras, all established in the months following the war. Big music took shape in the form of corporate competition for customer loyalty in the record shops and over the radio. The airwaves in the United States theoretically belonged to the people and practically belonged to big business. Elsewhere the national broadcasting services created multiple full-time orchestras to service their various regions, among them the BBC Symphony Orchestra, those of the Deutsche Rundfunk (in the East, West, North, and Southeast), Radio France, and the Australian and Canadian broadcasting companies. The number of employed orchestral musicians roughly quadrupled.

The philharmonic was "highbrow," to use a term considered by Lawrence W. Levine in his influential *Highbrow/Lowbrow: The Emergence of Cultural Hierarchy in America* (1988). What is now called the sacralization of art music set in, with the orchestra as its standard bearer.

Bigger than baseball

The "great symphonic boom" began in the 1930s and lasted some five decades. In a 1953 essay, the most interesting of American music critics, Virgil Thomson, offered a catalog of statistics on how Americans took their leisure, listing national expenditures of $45 million on orchestra music (paid "at the gate" in the form of 300

Signature sonorities

Amsterdam: Royal Concertgebouw Orchestra. The warm, intimate sound of the hall itself, allowing the players not to force. Delicate, nuanced string playing sometimes called silver or velvety. Long association with the symphonies of Bruckner and Mahler. Sophisticated percussion. *Listen to* Mahler: Symphony No. 3 in D Minor, movt. I: Kräftig, Entschieden, cond. Bernard Haitink (Philips, 1966).

Berlin Philharmonic Orchestra. Voluptuous, highly refined readings, typically ascribed to Herbert von Karajan's instruction that left-hand vibrato was to begin before the bow touched the string. Loud, throaty brass. *Listen to* Sibelius: Symphony No. 5, movt. III: Allegro molto, cond. Herbert von Karajan (Deutsche Grammophon, 1965).

Chicago Symphony Orchestra. The "Chicago brass": a grandeur and technical perfection ascribed variously to the conductor Fritz Reiner and to the principal trumpet player, Adolph Herseth, and tubist, Arnold Jacobs. A Facebook fan-site calls it "the single most awesome brass section of any professional orchestra," and Chicago remains the locus of choice for professional students of brass instruments. *Listen to* Richard Strauss: *Also sprach Zarathustra*, cond. Georg Solti (Decca, 1975).

Cleveland Orchestra. Technical perfection, careful attention to dynamic contrasts, studied orchestral counterpoint often called transparent, and a lean, European sonority. George Szell drilled every nuance of his readings into the players during relentless rehearsals, with trademark results to be heard on an impressive discography. *Listen to* Dvořák: Slavonic Dance in B Major, op. 72, no. 1, cond. George Szell (Columbia [now Sony Classical], 1965).

London Symphony Orchestra. High-spirited extrovert readings, celebrated soloists in the ranks (James Galway, flute; Gervase de Peyer, clarinet; Barry Tuckwell, horn). Flexibility in adapting to its many distinguished visiting conductors. The London Symphony Chorus; film scores (*Braveheart, Harry Potter*). *Listen to* Elgar: *The Dream of Gerontius*, end of part I, "Proficiscere, anima Christiana / Go forth, in the name of Angels and Archangels," cond. Colin Davis (LSO Live, 2006).

Philadelphia Orchestra. Seamless string phrasing (the "Philadelphia sound"; "those fabulous Philadelphians"). Often said to be a response to the dry acoustic of the orchestra's former home, the Philadelphia Academy of Music; accomplished in part by subtle overlapping of bow changes. *Listen to* Tchaikovsky: Symphony No. 5 in E Minor, op. 64, movt. III: Valse, cond. Riccardo Muti (EMI, 1992).

Vienna Philharmonic. Instruments unique to Vienna. The Vienna oboe and rotary-valve brass are small-bored with a delicate, focused quality. String instruments belong to the orchestra, not the players, and thus are handed down from generation to generation. The purity and ongoing tradition of the sound was long attributed, also, to gender and racial purity of the white European male musicians. *Listen to* Beethoven: Symphony No. 7 in A Major, op. 72, movt. III: Presto, cond. Carlos Kleiber (Deutsche Grammophon, 1976).

million admissions), baseball $40 million, horse and dog racing $38 million, professional football $9 million. Additionally $60 million was spent annually on classical records. Thomson counted 938 symphony orchestras in the United States. Music in general (teaching, performance, instrument manufacture) was the sixth largest American industry, after automobiles but before steel.

The boom was international in scope. For the most part the old European orchestras recovered within a few years from the rubble of World War II, so anxious were patrons and governments to resume their cultural programs as proof of returning normalcy. Orchestras based on European models had sprung up long before in colonial capitals from North Africa to Shanghai and Hong Kong; the 1950s saw healthy symphony orchestras emerge all across Asia, for instance the Central Philharmonic Orchestra of Beijing (1956) and the Seoul Philharmonic (1957). Tokyo alone, building on the success of the NHK (Radio) Orchestra (1926), boasted more than a half-dozen professional orchestras, with the halls, festivals, and music schools that have traditionally characterized the world's great musical capitals. The thirst for orchestral music in the Asian markets of the 1970s and '80s was all but unquenchable.

At the end of the twentieth century and into the new millennium, the institution was surely in crisis, under assault from changes in urban demographics, from electronics, from what appeared to be an aging audience biased toward a repertoire frozen in an irrelevant past. The orchestras fought back, stumbled forward, and more often than not succeeded in adapting to the new ways, sustained by constituents loathe to lose their philharmonic. The music center was, after all, a matter of civic prestige, on the order of stadiums and airports. The orchestra was, as always, its principal resident company.

The question was the fit. Had classical music, that of the orchestra, become a matter of what Theodor Adorno called "regressive listening," controlled by puerile motives generated in corporate headquarters? Or had the iPod and Internet put the orchestra on everybody's playlists?

Chapter 2
Musicians

It is a precarious career. The orchestral musician is both artist and artisan, métiers not always easy to reconcile. For much of orchestral history the pay has been by honorarium or desultory wage, and from multiple employers. The hierarchies are formal, long-standing, and not far removed from feudal ways. Inequalities are built into the music itself, where violinists play nearly every measure while trumpet players may have, in a work of Haydn or Schubert, only a few notes. Much of the work is repetitive. A good third of a big orchestra's players may sit out some portion of the concert. Orchestras routinely confound established principles of management and labor.

Still it is the hundred players onstage who actually set the sound waves in motion. They choose to be there, and would not have gone through the rigors of training and audition that got them to the stage had they been able to imagine anything else. They may be fatigued by the rigors of the season but are seldom so jaded as the caricaturists suggest. Fine ensemble playing, being a negotiated outcome, keeps the mind sharp with its demand for split-second response to conditions of the moment, whether one has played a work once or a hundred times.

In 2010–11 the base pay in a fifty-two-week American orchestra was something on the order of $100,000, higher at the top, of course, and falling dramatically for organizations with shorter seasons. Per-service engagements paid $200 and less: multiply by two or three rehearsals and one or two concerts to come up with a week's wages. An orchestral musician today is thus apt to juggle contracts while teaching in the studio and driving long distances. (Musicians who play in multiple per-service orchestras are said to be members of the Freeway Philharmonic.) Some play in early music, new music, and chamber ensembles, acquiring an encyclopedic command of styles and options.

Musicians come in families, since becoming an orchestral player is often a family decision. The Tolbecques of Belgium sent four children to seek their musical fortunes in Paris at the time the Conservatory Orchestra was getting under way, fostering a dynasty that included Auguste Tolbecque, *fils*, the great restorer of old violins. Dennis Brain, the English player who popularized the French horn concertos of Mozart, was the grandson, son, and nephew of professional horn players (and his older brother was an oboist). In the United States, John Corigliano Sr. was concertmaster of the New York Philharmonic and Corigliano Jr., a distinguished composer of music for symphony orchestra (Symphony No. 1, 1991; music for *The Red Violin*, 1999). Likewise Alan Gilbert, conductor since 2009 of the New York Philharmonic, grew up in the milieu: both parents, Michael Gilbert and Yoko Takebe, were in the Philharmonic. His sister, Jennifer Gilbert, is concertmaster of the Orchestre de Lyon. The elder Gilbert runs Ensemble Eroica, anchored in Memphis and promoting classical music throughout west Tennessee.

Lineage from teachers to student matters, too. Harp players trace their technique back to Carlos Salzedo or Marcel Grandjany and the French just as surely as ballet masters have family trees rooted at the barre in Napoleon's court. The exceptional American school of viola playing coalesced at the Curtis Institute of Music around Louis Bailly and William Primrose, both immigrants. Among their descendants were Joseph de Pasquale, who left his principal chair in the Boston Symphony Orchestra to come to the Philadelphia Orchestra and Curtis; and Roberto Díaz, de Pasquale's successor in both duties, who went on to become president of Curtis. Díaz plays the "Primrose" viola (Antonio and Hieronymus Amati, ca. 1600) and has recorded Primrose's crowd-pleasing recital repertoire: Liszt's *La Campanella*, the Villa-Lobos *Bachianas brasileiras* No. 5, the Adagio from Bizet's *L'Arlésienne* (Naxos 2006).

Musicians simultaneously acquire the technique and the tradition of their instruments at the schools of music and conservatories established to supply the world's orchestras and opera houses. The modern professional curriculum includes also career management and strategies for preventing occupational injury. Graduates begin their careers where opportunity calls, auditioning wherever they can. Orchestras now follow a "blind" audition policy, where at least in the early rounds the player sits behind a screen while a panel consisting of music director, general manager, and representative players evaluates set pieces. This system has in large measure replaced conductor autocracy and various forms of patronage where empowered player-teachers saw to it that their students got the work. As equal opportunity has extended into the audition process, labor unions have relaxed their traditional opposition to players imported from abroad.

Players are first engaged with probationary contracts and go on to achieve tenure through a review process, which often includes a vote of the other players. A typical orchestra career lasts twenty-five or thirty years.

A central concern of the professional musician is the need to acquire suitable instruments. Orchestral quality wind instruments start in the $3,000 range; harps at $12,500 and up. A good vintage Heckel bassoon begins at $22,000. Violin-family instruments at the orchestral level are in the $50,000-and-above range, not including bows and cases. A good nineteenth-century violin by the Gand and Bernadel luthiers of Paris might be had for $25,000. In 2010 a Nicolò Amati, 1765, sold for $576,000; a French violin by J. B. Vuillaume, ca. 1865, for $210,000 in New York. Virtually every orchestra player owns multiple instruments.

In 2003 the New Jersey Symphony Orchestra purchased thirty rare stringed instruments, including several by Stradivarius, from the collection of the eccentric entrepreneur Herbert Axelrod, reasoning that this "Golden Age" collection would not only improve the sound of the orchestra but also attract artists, patrons, and donors. Neeme Järvi took the conductor's job there owing in part to the collection. Questions soon surfaced about the worth of the instruments, eventually established to be about $17 million; the authenticity and rightful ownership of some of them was publicly questioned. The collection was ultimately sold for $20 million to investment bankers, who agreed to leave most of the instruments to be played by the New Jersey musicians through 2012.

Democracy

The founders of the philharmonic societies were children of the Enlightenment. They took it as a given that the proper form of government was decision-making by ballot of members. Their constitutions and bylaws provided for annual meetings of the full company and ways to resolve disputes. Other provisions outlined the duties of each officer (including the conductor), appointment procedures, and mandatory retirement ages. The members were prepared to do the work of administering the concert series, either gratis or for a small fee.

As symphony orchestras grew more popular and more worldly, they added non-musician staff: a lawyer, a physician, a bookkeeper. As they undertook routine tours and weekly contract services, the managing fellows found themselves so frequently absent from their central duty—playing in the concerts—that by the middle of the twentieth century virtually every orchestra had a professional manager. Musicians, formerly electors and share-holders, became the rank and file.

Orchestral musicians had long been organized for social benevolence. Pension funds and widows-and-orphans funds were in place in the earliest days of public concerts. The Burgtheater performance of Haydn's *Creation* was to benefit the local Musicians' Widows Fund; a Society of British and Foreign Musicians was established in London in 1822 "to provide a fund for the relief of its members during sickness; to assist in the support of those who, by old age or unavoidable calamity may become unable to follow the profession; and to allow a certain sum at the death of a member or a member's wife." It was a natural step, in some cities, to join the trade-union movement; from one point of view players had always been apprentices, journeymen, and master craftsmen.

Gender and race

European white male musicians dominated the profession until toward the end of the twentieth century. Women harpists found employment in the orchestras but not full membership. Here and there a person of color was to be noted onstage and enjoyed public welcome on grounds of his exoticism. With rare exceptions, demonstrating how archconservative they had grown with age, orchestras followed and did not lead societal change.

The slow assimilation of women into the orchestra began in the American Midwest, where the Cleveland Orchestra had women members from its first season in 1918–19. Doriot Anthony Dwyer was appointed principal flute in the Boston Symphony Orchestra in 1952 to breathless, often tasteless, coverage by the press: *Time* described her as "perky, dimpled"; the Springfield paper as "30 and pretty." The *Globe* headline read: "Woman Crashes Boston Symphony" and went on to note how the new principal "dressed well without aiming at spectacular effect, and her lipstick, though generously applied, is the right shade for her coloring."

More than a decade later Leonard Bernstein chose Orin O'Brien, a doublebassist, to break the gender barrier in the New York Philharmonic, on which occasion a reporter observed that "Miss O'Brien is as curvy as the double bass she plays."

Breaking the gender barrier took much longer in Berlin and Vienna. For the 1982–83 season of the Berlin Philharmonic, Herbert von Karajan engaged the clarinetist Sabine Meyer as the first woman member of the orchestra; after her probationary period the musicians' vote on her tenure was four favoring and seventy-three opposing. That she was "not retained" was explained as a question of her tone not blending with the others. Meyer went on to become one of the few brand-name woodwind players on the concerto circuit.

2. Doriot Anthony Dwyer, newly appointed principal flute and one of only two women in the Boston Symphony Orchestra, is introduced to the players, October 1952.

The Vienna Philharmonic's highly publicized position, taken "with staggering candor," was to the effect (a half century after World War II) that ethnic and gender purity was at the root of the orchestra's artistic superiority. "[Men] carry secrets that are involved with music and tones, just like in Australian aboriginal or Indian cultures where men play certain instruments, and not the women."

The admission of women would be "gambling with the emotional unity that we currently have."

"Pregnancy brings problems. It brings disorder."

"They distract men. Not the older women. No one gives a damn about the older ones. It is the younger ones. In a monastery it is the same."

"The Vienna Philharmonic would also never take a Japanese or such" as this would "by appearances put in question the noble character of Viennese culture."

In 1995 the representation of women in American and British Orchestras was about 33 percent; in German-speaking countries half that. The largest percentage of women tended to be found in the lower-paying orchestras. In 2009 most of the major orchestras in the United States were at about 33 percent; London and Boston at about 25 percent, and the Berlin Philharmonic at 14 percent. Vienna was still in last place, with a single female player, the harpist Charlotte Baltzereit. "This instrument is so far at the edge of the orchestra," it had been said in Vienna, "that it doesn't disturb our emotional unity."

The doublebassist Ortiz Walton, later a leader in African American studies, broke the color barrier in both Buffalo (1954) and Boston (1957), where the trustees promised to cancel tour appearances in any city that denied him lodging with his colleagues. In

1970 Eugene Ormandy appointed two African Americans in their twenties, Renard Edwards and Booker T. Rowe, to the Philadelphia Orchestra. (The Philadelphia that season had 107 players and a starting salary of $15,000.) "They were chosen entirely because of their musical abilities," said Ormandy, who was publicly characterized as oblivious to the questions of race but, in the back room, as a bigot. The motivation in Philadelphia had almost certainly come from New York, where Leonard Bernstein, anything but bigoted, was called to testify before the New York City Commission on Human Rights in a 1969 discrimination suit brought against the Philharmonic by Earl Madison, a cellist, and J. Arthur Davis, a doublebassist. A ruling favorable to the Philharmonic eventually came down, though the panel complained of discriminatory practices in hiring students of the players as extras and substitutes. In 1969 there was one African American member of the Philharmonic, the violinist Sanford Allen; in 2009, none.

Union labor

Orchestral musicians syndicated much as the medieval guilds had done, keeping counterparts in touch both regionally and across Europe. Their organizations argued for favorable wage scales and benefits, and established positions in early debates on performance rights and on foreign competition. Benevolent and mutual aid societies were locally based, almost invariably assuming social equality of their members in terms of rights and entitlements. In 1896 the American Federation of Labor (AFL) oversaw the linking of local musician syndicates into the American Federation of Musicians (AFM), numbering some 3,000 members at its foundation.

Under the notorious Chicago boss James Petrillo, the AFM championed working musicians, mostly outside the classical sphere, in nationwide maneuvers seen variously as brilliant, ruffian, gangsterist, and communist. His most notorious action was the strike called against the recording companies in 1942–44, hence during wartime, over who paid and who received royalties for record sales. "ALL RECORDING STOPS TODAY," trumpeted *DownBeat*'s headline on August 1, 1942: "Prexy Petrillo has not backed down [from] his claim that recording was ruining the jobs of 60 percent of the AFM membership and that he meant to do something about it." A more direct effect on American classical musicians came after a second strike against the record companies in 1948, since the settlement established the Recording Industry Music Performance Trust Fund, an ingenious mechanism by which record profits were channeled—through the union—back to musicians as payment for live public services in their communities.

Whatever its successes in the industry at large the AFM was not especially popular with orchestral musicians, who preferred being represented in contract negotiations by their own players' committees instead of officers of the AFM local. To address this problem, players organized the International Conference of Symphony and Opera Musicians, ICSOM, in 1962, representing the 4,000 or so players in the fifty-one AFM orchestras then in the United States. ICSOM publishes current contract information for its member orchestras and a robust trade magazine called *Senza Sordino* (the instruction in an orchestra score for "unmuted"), both on the Web. The Regional Orchestra Players Association, ROPA, was established along similar lines in 1982.

Orchestral musicians remain closely federated and powerfully represented. The success of the union movement in advancing the salaries of working musicians and addressing abusive practices is undeniable. The propriety of union representation for artist musicians is nevertheless sharply debated within the profession and without. "It made sense for coal miners like my grandfather," wrote the Republican blogger David Frum, suggesting in 2011 that the relationship of Detroit Symphony musicians with "Big Labor" was "manifestly absurd." But ongoing struggle to achieve economic viability is certain, to say nothing of the challenge of keeping live orchestras in the pit on Broadway and London's West

End. "Keep Music Alive" is the current motto of the British version of the Musicians' Union.

Contracts

A modern negotiated contract typically provides a base pay for a season defined in weeks: in Dallas, $90,000 for fifty-two weeks; in St. Louis, $81,000 for forty-three weeks; in Oregon, $43,000 for thirty-eight weeks. An Electronic Media Guarantee clause represents a stipend added to salary checks to compensate players for distribution of their work over the air or on record, whether or not that happens. The fine print of the ratification agreements posted in the United States since 2009 is a sobering catalog of reduced seasons and dramatically lowered benefits as executives struggled to reconcile terrifying levels of deficit alongside declining endowment values. The Charlotte Symphony Orchestra, explaining in September 2009 why contractual goals had not been met, listed woes including:

> economic downturn and the lack of a substantive endowment and small donor base, [and] an accumulated deficit of over $3 million for an annual budget of $8 million. In addition, the CSO faced further losses for the current season when the Arts and Science Council reduced its grant to the CSO by over $1 million, Opera Carolina postponed a fall production, and the county school system eliminated arts field trips for elementary students. The elimination of the opera and education performances result in a loss of three weeks of work for the orchestra.

The dire financial situation of orchestras, more or less global by then, led to one after another contract proposal deemed unacceptable by the musicians, who felt themselves left with no other option but to strike. A strike in Cleveland lasted less than a day; in Seattle a strike was authorized but the players settled beforehand. The situation in Detroit in 2010–11 led to a six-month walkout.

Strikes by arts workers are unusually abrasive, since they bring to the fore harsh facts of life—the relatively low value placed on rank-and-file artists, for instance—and appear to come at the expense of donors and civic boosters. "If we lose the DSO, we lose Detroit," a piano teacher wailed. The players invariably, if temporarily, lose stature. And if the orchestra goes out of business, the road back is uninviting. Hawaii lost its professional orchestra twice in a decade; in April 2011 a Symphony Exploratory Committee bought the assets of the Honolulu Symphony Orchestra and reached a three-year agreement with symphony musicians that embraces a good deal of wait-and-see. Through much of 2011, the Orquestra Sinfônica Brasileira (Brazilian Symphony Orchestra) in Rio de Janeiro—a historic orchestra long associated with the distinguished conductor Eleazar de Carvalho—was frozen in a bitter labor dispute that erupted when the players were ordered by management to undergo "performance evaluations" as "part of a continuous process of improvement and artistic evolution" to make a "great orchestra . . . even better." This struggle, too, closely watched by orchestral labor and management the world over, left the usual community devastation, including a canceled season and universal disgruntlement.

In the United Kingdom, by sharp contrast with these labor practices (and excepting the state-owned BBC Symphony Orchestra and its siblings), there have been virtually no ongoing contracts for orchestral musicians since the 1950s, per-service agreements having taken their place. A 2007 Musicians' Union report on orchestral pay made "pretty dismal reading" as it described "not much glamour, not too much pay, and little time for anything else" as orchestral players scrambled to make a living. A member of the Royal Liverpool Symphony Orchestra earned about £24,000 ($36,000) per year, sharply below the average full-time worker's income for the nation at large. Elsewhere in Europe (and at the BBC), much of the orchestral enterprise is, one way or another, state controlled. And while the musicians enjoy the considerable privileges and guarantees of modern European civil servants, they are by the same token subject to the same constant buffetings and work actions that affect teachers, transportation workers, and the post office.

The daily concerns of the orchestral musician run from the conspicuous oversupply of young players—Indiana University's School of Music alone graduates a dozen trombone majors a year—to the new field of arts medicine, addressing issues from repetitive stress syndromes to preventable hearing loss. Career growth and satisfaction for long-term players is much at issue, with interesting proposals on the table for sabbatical leaves and perhaps seat exchanges with other orchestras, both domestic and foreign. And then there are the unexpected headaches, like inconsistent airline policies on instruments in the cabin. Different versions of language concerning this matter were passed by the U.S. Senate and House of Representatives as part of the FAA (Federal Aviation Authority) Reauthorization Act of 2011. Most orchestral instruments would be allowed in overhead bins or purchased seats.

Musicians develop a knack for turning the uncertainties into opportunity. Jorja Fleezanis, the popular violinist who retired after a long career at the front of the San Francisco Symphony and Minnesota Orchestra, is one of those orchestral players who see their careers, the opportunity to live face-to-face with the giants of music past and present, as a providential gift. Hers was, she reminds us, the best seat in the house. She left to become a professor at Indiana, where she meant to show how gratifying her orchestral career had been. "It's not about how many jobs [the students] will get, but how to be good citizens in the profession."

Chapter 3
Venue

Only a handful of the birthplace venues for concert music are still in use. The historic Gewandhaus in Leipzig was replaced in 1884, and that building was subsequently lost in the Allied bombings of February 1944. The Hanover Square Rooms were demolished in 1900. The concert hall of the Paris Conservatoire, 2*bis* rue du Conservatoire, where Beethoven was unveiled to the Parisians and Berlioz's *Symphonie fantastique* born, today serves the national Conservatory of Dramatic Art, and though restored to its general appearance of the 1840s is so dampened to accommodate spoken voice that the celebrated acoustic is lost.

Among the noble products of municipal industry of the late nineteenth century the four great concert venues are the "Golden Hall" of the Vienna Musikverein (1870), the Concertgebouw in Amsterdam (1888), Carnegie Hall (1891), and Boston Symphony Hall (1900). Two others that typically make the top-ten lists are the Schauspielhaus in Berlin, now called the Konzerthaus (1821), and the Teatro Colón in Buenos Aires (1908). Their reputations rest largely on their acoustics, measured in terms of audience and performer satisfaction and, increasingly, by scientific means. But invariably, too, they are cultural landmarks, both geographically and historically.

Venues of less perfect sound may be equally pleasing: take as an example the Great Hall of the St. Petersburg Philharmonic, with its splendid colonnades and gleaming cream-and-gilt décor overhung by eight great crystal chandeliers. This wonderful room was completed in 1839 as an Assembly Hall of the Nobles, a gentry club for receptions and dancing, with canopied platform, festoons, potted greenery. The local philharmonic society engaged it for concerts early on. Here Liszt played to 3,000, including the czar and his court, in 1842; Berlioz conducted his works in both 1847 and, in what were essentially his last public appearances, the winter of 1867–68; Mahler led his Fifth Symphony in 1907, mightily impressing the young Stravinsky. In 1859 it became the home of the first professional orchestra concerts given by Rubinstein's Russian Musical Society and soon of the modern St. Petersburg Philharmonic (1883). Here, too, occurred Yevgeny Mravinsky's fifty-year run with the Leningrad Philharmonic—making of the Great Hall a temple to Tchaikovsky and Shostakovitch; and here the Iron Curtain was effectively rent by the Boston Symphony Orchestra in 1956, at the dawn of the Age of Cultural Diplomacy.

Great houses anchor a city. They afford the public satisfaction and pride, and visitors fond memories. The visionary Andrew Carnegie remarked, as he laid the cornerstone for the hall that would later carry his name, "It is built to stand for ages, and during these ages it is probable that this hall will intertwine itself with the history of our country." In their bowels are precious libraries of scores and parts often marked with generations of performance tradition. There are archives of concert programs and photographs and live recordings, and warehouses of unwieldy instruments, ranging from contrabassoons and harps to church bells and wind machines.

The historic halls are typically rectangular with seating for 3,000 or less—the "shoebox" model. A pipe organ sometimes fills the far wall, rising above the orchestra. The shoebox acoustic allows a sound to resonate long enough for warmth but to decay before clouding the music, something on the order of between 1.8 and 2.2 seconds.

Noted orchestral venues

	Built/ Renovated	Seats	Cost	Architect / Acoustician
Vienna: Grosser Musikvereinssaal	1870	2,044		Theophil Hansen
Amsterdam: Concertgebouw	1888	2,037		Adolf Leonard van Gendt
New York: Carnegie Hall	1891 ren. 1991	2,804	$1 million	William Burnet Tuthill
Boston: Symphony Hall	1900	2,625		McKim, Mead, and White; Wallace Clement Sabine
Chicago: Orchestra Hall	1904 ren. 1997	2,522		Daniel H. Burnham
Cleveland: Severance Hall	1931 ren. 1958, 1998	2,100	$7 million	Walker and Weeks
Berlin: Philharmonie Grosser Saal	1963	2,440	DM13.5 million	Hans Scharoun

	Built/ Reno-vated	Seats	Cost	Architect / Acoustician
London: Barbican Hall, Barbican Centre	1982	1,949	£161 million (full facility)	Chamberlain, Powell, and Bon; acoustics ren. Larry Kirkegaard (1994) and Caruso St. John (2001)
Birmingham: Symphony Hall	1991	2,262	£30 million	Percy Thomas Partnership, Renton Howard Wood; Russell Johnson, Artec Consultants Inc.
Tokyo: Opera City Concert Hall (Takemitsu Memorial)	1997	1,632	¥77 billion (full facility)	Takahiko Yanagisawa, TAK Associated Architects; Leo Beranek and Takenaka Research and Development Institute
Los Angeles: Walt Disney Concert Hall	2003	2,265	$130 million	Frank Gehry; Nagata Acoustics

	Built/ Reno- vated	Seats	Cost	Architect / Acoustician
Paris: Philharmonie, Cité de la Musique	2014	2,400	£170 million	Jean Nouvel, Brigitte Métra; Marshall Day Acoustics, Nagata Acoustics

Resident orchestras adapt to the positive and negative features of their venue, with the result that their true characteristic sound can only be heard at home.

In the recent "vineyard" model, terraces of seats surround the orchestra, offering advantages of intimacy for players and listeners alike and a good space for the chorus. Herbert von Karajan was an early partisan of this arrangement, as reflected in the Berlin Philharmonie (1963) built during his tenure—not least because it affords a front view of the conductor at work. Dual-use halls, typically for theatre and concert music, are converted into their orchestral figuration by creating some form of chamber framed by the proscenium and walled in from the offstage area and the flyhouse.

The reputation of a concert venue is in the end quite subjective, a matter of how artists and seasoned listeners feel about it for reasons that go well beyond how the music sounds there.

Vienna—Amsterdam—Boston

Acoustics in the rooms where the first concert societies proffered their wares were catch-as-catch-can, and for much of the nineteenth century the dominant problem was how to accommodate an ever-increasing number of players and singers onstage. In the last quarter of the century orchestral size stabilized, making possible the planning and construction of venues that have retained their purpose ever since. The classic concert halls took their identity as temples of art seriously indeed, incorporating names of the great composers in the painted décor and allegorical statues in the niches.

In Vienna the land was donated by the emperor Franz Joseph to the Gesellschaft der Musikfreunde, or the Musikverein, for a new building to be located near the imperial palace within the Ringstrasse. The larger of the rooms, the Grosse Musikvereinssaal, is long and narrow, its loges hung perpendicular to the room instead of being arranged in the opera-house horseshoe. Everything is gilded: coffered ceiling, organ gallery, lintels, balconies, and the statues that support them. This was Karajan's home before (and after) Berlin, where Bernstein did his best late-career conducting, site of the New Year's Day waltz concerts.

The corporation formed to bring a concert venue, or Concertgebouw, to Amsterdam had at the start no orchestra, only a piece of land. Even that was beyond the city in a marsh, requiring more than 2,000 forty-foot pilings to stabilize a foundation. But the urban planning was good: the Concertgebouw complimented the Rijksmuseum (1885) alongside the Museumplein, now surrounded by museums on every side. It opened in 1889, and the orchestra that went with it was first heard a few months later. Orchestra and house were managed together until 1953, when the players organized into a collective. A $21-million renovation to address the rotting foundation was begun in the 1980s and completed just in time for the 100th anniversary.

The legendary perfection of the room rests not only on its unusually live acoustic, but also on the view from the house toward the orchestra, which sits on a gently lifted platform with a steep amphitheater of seats and the pipeworks of a fine Dutch organ behind; the musicians take the stage by coming down the steps of the

35

amphitheater. On the walls of the audience chamber and balconies are painted the names of the great composers as reckoned locally, from Sweelinck to Ravel. The sound of the Royal Concertgebouw Orchestra is certainly a function of the room but also of the traditional life tenures for its conductors: fifty years for Willem Mengelberg and roughly the same for Eduard van Beinum and Bernard Haitink.

Boston's Symphony Hall (1900), modeled after the Concertgebouw and the Leipzig Gewandhaus, was unique in having had an acoustical consultant, Wallace Sabine, a Harvard professor of physics and pioneer of room acoustics. (The unit by which sound absorption is measured is called the sabin in his honor.) The acoustic success of the hall is thought to be a function of its box shape with inward-sloping walls, shallow balconies that reduce sound traps beneath, and reflection from the columns, niches, and statues above the balconies. Subsequent renovations, including a new Aeolian-Skinner organ in 1949 and reopening the clerestories shuttered down during the blackouts of World War II, went out of their way to preserve the specifications of the room. In 2006, when the stage floor had to be replaced, the wood and its tongue-and-groove placement were duplicated and replicas of the original nails manufactured for hammering in by hand. The main floor of the room is dramatically repurposed with cabaret seating for the summer and holiday concerts of the Boston Pops, without much harming the basic acoustic.

Carnegie Hall

Andrew Carnegie and his bride, Louise, en route in 1887 from New York to their estate in Scotland, befriended the twenty-five-year-old conductor Walter Damrosch aboard ship. By the end of the summer Damrosch, who had just concluded his second season as conductor of the New York Symphony Society, had talked them into his notion of a new hall for uptown Manhattan. Carnegie proceeded to buy up the land between Fifty-sixth and Fifty-seventh streets along Seventh Avenue, and there erected a building with a 2,800-seat main hall, a recital hall below seating 1,200, and a 250-seat chamber music room to the side. Upstairs were rooms for lectures, receptions, and lodge meetings. On opening night, May 5, 1891, after the inevitable crush of carriages untangled itself, Damrosch led Beethoven's Leonore Overture No. 3, Tchaikovsky appeared on stage to lead his Festival Coronation march, and the seldom heard Te Deum of Berlioz concluded the program.

Carnegie Hall was of splendid appearance, with glamorous curving balconies and the gilt-and-red décor of the Beaux-Arts style. But it owed its conspicuous success to the caliber of the artists it attracted from the first: all the great pianists, Ravel and Rachmaninov, Arthur Rubinstein and Vladimir Horowitz, Van Cliburn on his triumphant return from Moscow—likewise the world's leading singers, violinsts, and cellists. At "An Experiment in Modern Music" there on February 12, 1924, Paul Whiteman premiered Gershwin's *Rhapsody in Blue*, maneuvering jazz into highbrow culture. As home to the New York Philharmonic and as the recording venue for the NBC Symphony under Toscanini, Carnegie Hall was rivaled in national standing only by the Metropolitan Opera House.

But in 1955 the Philharmonic announced its defection to occupy, with the Met, the New York State Theatre, and the Juilliard School of Music, the new Lincoln Center, an urban redevelopment project to replace more than a dozen blocks of tenements (the site, in fact, of *West Side Story*). As the result of losing its anchor client, Carnegie Hall would be demolished and replaced by an office tower. The violinist Isaac Stern proceeded to alert and then mobilize the world's artists in an effort to preserve the venue. The national patrimony, he argued, was at stake. By 1962 the building had been sold to the city of New York and was named a National Historic Landmark. A 1981 master plan described a ten-year program of renovations successfully finished in time for the hall's centenary in 1991.

By the end of the twentieth century the great halls of the nineteenth were in dire need of modern conveniences for the public spaces (proper toilet facilities, good food-service options, parking) and the company (notably, women's dressing rooms). Many needed to accommodate longer seasons for their orchestras and thus find new spaces for their other tenants. Whole campuses on the order of Lincoln Center took shape, for instance the Portland (Oregon) Center for the Performing Arts (1984), anchored by a stunning remodel of the ornate Paramount Theater as a concert venue. Out of Orchestra Hall in Chicago, a Daniel Burnham masterpiece of 1904, was coaxed the $110 million Symphony Center (1997), with new rehearsal spaces, offices, and restaurant. The opulent Severance Hall in Cleveland was reopened in 2000 after a $36 million, two-year renovation that included construction of a five-story administrative building behind, removal and refurbishment of the E. M. Skinner pipe organ, and thoroughgoing overhaul of the audience areas.

The acousticians

The field of architectural acoustics, and the idea that a concert hall would be the joint work of architects and acousticians, was largely the accomplishment of Leo Beranek, founder of Bolt, Beranek and Newman. After wartime experience designing noise reduction for military aircraft, he remained in the nascent field of acoustic engineering, teaching at MIT and there writing the classic textbook in the field. Beranek's *Concert Halls and Opera Houses: Music, Acoustics, and Architecture* (1962, 2nd ed. 2004) analyzed the highly reputed concert halls throughout the world with an understanding that scientific inquiry was only a part of the transaction: the pleasure of listening involved taste and tradition as well. His theories of ideal resonance and decay times for orchestra halls gained wide acceptance, as did his techniques of calibrating and adjusting the behavior of concert venues. This was accomplished mostly by the positioning of reflective (or for some purposes absorptive) panels about the house to perfect how the sound waves traveled from the individual musician to the listeners' ears. "Tuning" a venue with science became a work of art.

Contemporary architecture and engineering have also been greatly successful in curbing the incursion of outside noise into the sound chamber. New auditoriums are now routinely suspended within an outer shell, sealed from ambient highways, railroads, and flight paths. A less attractive confrontation of man and nature occurred at the Saratoga Performing Arts Center in upstate New York, host of annual visits from the Philadelphia Orchestra, where Eugene Ormandy ordered a dam built to quell the waterfall noise from a nearby creek.

Between the science and its application there have been spectacular failures. Philharmonic Hall, now Avery Fisher Hall, in Lincoln Center was one. It opened in October 1962 to mixed reviews that went consistently downhill thereafter. The failure is now attributed to adjustments demanded late in the construction phase in order to permit a larger number of seats, and to a flaw in Beranek's theory of initial sound decay. "My dream of a great hall and my reputation as an acoustician both appear to be going up in smoke," he wrote. Subsequent adjustments on small and large scales helped a little, but in 2005 the Philharmonic and its landlord agreed on a $300-million program to gut and rebuild the chamber, part of a billion-dollar redevelopment of Lincoln Center already under way.

Beranek's successors included Russell Johnson, founder of the Artec firm, whose masterpieces were the Morton H. Meyerson Symphony Center in Dallas (1989) and the orchestra halls in Birmingham, England, and Lucerne; and Cyril Harris, who consulted for the new Metropolitan Opera, the Kennedy Center, and the most successful of the efforts to remodel Avery Fisher Hall (1976). Silva Hall (1982) in the spectacular Hult Center for the Performing Arts in Eugene, Oregon, featured a new twist. When the city fathers balked at the cost of separate rooms for acoustic and amplified music, the architects, Hardy Holzman Pfeiffer Associates, put them in touch with the acoustician Christopher Jaffe, who proposed "electronic enhancement" (broadly speaking, artificial feedback from microphones and speakers) of the single environment to meet the needs of a classical orchestra. Halls in Anchorage, Alaska, and Nashville, Tennessee, adopted later generations of the technology.

Classical musicians were naturally and professionally skeptical. Technologically curious ones, like the pianist Garrick Ohlsson, were invited to experiment with the system: half a program on, half off. But the conductor Marin Alsop, on moving to Eugene, had it shut down for her concerts. "To rely on a sound technician for your balance," she said, "is completely antithetical to the role of a conductor." Nevertheless, "soundscape" controlled from a booth became the norm for nearly everything but classical music. An agonizing by-product is the amount of artificial resonance routinely engineered into classical music recordings since the 1990s.

Of the 100 leading halls in thirty-one countries Leo Beranek treated in the 2004 edition of his book, twenty-three are outside Europe and the United States, and thirty are new. No fewer than a dozen of them are found in Tokyo, more than in any other city.

Concert halls at the millennium

Walt Disney Hall in the Los Angeles Music Center, fourth home of the Los Angeles Philharmonic, opened in October 2003 after a fifteen-year gestation period. It was the most talked-about civic project of its era, object of delays and feuds between the celebrity architect Frank Gehry and the chief philanthropist, Eli Broad (of the builders Kaufmann Broad / KB Home). It was easily the most complex concert venue ever undertaken, and certainly the most expensive, coming in at $284 million (all costs, including the parking garage and 2006 settlement of subsequent lawsuits), nearly three times the original budget of $100 million.

When all was said and done there was little not to like. Fantasy sails of silver and white overlaid not just the Music Center but

3. Walt Disney Concert Hall, Los Angeles; Frank Gehry, architect, 2009.

downtown LA as a whole, met on the inside by tumbling stacks of organ pipes and the cascading vineyard terraces of seats. The acoustic properties, as designed by Minoru Nagata and his firm, were seductive—some say unparalleled. The philosophy of the performance chamber was largely that of the orchestra's executive director, Ernest Fleischmann, with roots in the design of the new Philharmonie in Berlin (1963). Fleischmann wanted every ticket holder to sense equal ownership of the concert, in terms especially of good sight lines and a sense of proximity for all. Players and conductors had stakes in the planning, but in the end "this was his dream," said Gehry, "and I was being entrusted with delivering that dream."

Disney Hall is an excellent case study of civic philharmonia in all its abrasive reality. One key figure was Dorothy Chandler, department store heiress and wife of the owner of the *Los Angeles Times,* easily the most powerful figure in the city's cultural life.

41

Already she had rescued the Hollywood Bowl (1951), hired and driven away—before he showed up to take the job—Georg Solti, engaged Zubin Mehta (1961), and overseen the construction and opening of the Philharmonic's third hall, Dorothy Chandler Pavilion (1964). Another was Fleischmann, whose arrival as general manager in 1969 shook everything up when he protested decision-making by "meatpackers, merchants, and housewives" and cast himself as executive producer, rewriting the script top to bottom and at length calling for the new hall.

The lead gift of $50 million came from Lillian Disney, Walt Disney's widow, in 1987. Within a year Fleischmann had seen to the choice of Gehry as architect. But the plans, at 30,000 pages, were thought unbuildable, and the region was enduring a steady assault from recession, urban unrest, and earthquake. By 1996 the only progress to be seen at the site was the new municipal parking garage. Then in short succession Gehry completed the dazzling Guggenheim Museum Bilbao in Spain (1997), and the orchestra, under its new conductor Esa-Pekka Salonen, triumphed abroad in better acoustics: "a voice," raved the Los Angeles reviewer Mark Swed, "the home crowd . . . never hears." A follow-up gift from the Disneys' daughter Diane, and high-profile fundraising by the mayor, Richard Riordan, broke the logjam. Six years later, the building, much as designed, was ready for occupancy, fine-tuning, and public debut.

Other halls of the period share similar stories. The handsome Kimmel Center in Philadelphia grew from a 1985 plan to replace the Academy of Music and struggled to its opening in 2001 (2,500 seats, $180 million). Here the acoustic design was by Russell Johnson's firm Artec, hence with adjustable panels everywhere and 100 "acoustical closets" that could be opened and closed according to the circumstance. The dramatic shape and color of the room, evoking the look of a cello, enchants listeners before they hear a note of music. When the music starts, however, the questions begin, with some competent observers declaring the result a failure.

Not one but two new orchestra halls grace Miami, Florida. The 2,200-seat Knight Concert Hall in the Adrienne Arsht Center, 2006, was designed by the Argentinian architect César Pelli with acoustics by Russell Johnson. It is the home to the Cleveland Orchestra during the annual Miami Residency, a program begun in 2007. The other anchoring orchestra of the Arsht Center has been Michael Tilson Thomas's New World Symphony, an academy for early-career instrumentalists based in Miami Beach. In January 2011, the New World Center, another opus of Frank Gehry and his Disney Hall associates, opened after a contentious face-off between architect and city planners over parking lots and tropical landscaping. At only 756 seats, the concert room features "arena" wrap-around seating and fixed acoustics. The acoustic sails hanging above the orchestra allow for visual projections, and outdoors there is an enormous Projection Wall to take what is happening inside to those in the park. It was inaugurated with a new work by the British composer Thomas Adès, *Polaris*, with video by Tal Rosner. For the late-night Pulse concerts, the room is transformed into an atmosphere Michael Tilson Thomas calls "clubby." The cost was $160 million.

Summer and outdoor festivals

The summer festivals descend in large measure from long-standing leisure pastimes in Europe: taking the waters, gaming, and enjoying pops and proms in Vichy and Deauville, Baden-Baden and Bath. Even in their informal stages, they were crucial means of post-season livelihood for orchestral players. The Proms, eight weeks of concerts in London's Albert Hall, reach back to 1895 and are a direct descendant of walk-about quadrille concerts from the nineteenth-century pleasure gardens. Prommers, as they are called, line up at the rate of 1,000 per night to buy the cheap day-of-concert tickets.

The Strasbourg Music Festival was established in 1932 by a philharmonic society of long standing; the Lucerne Festival, by Toscanini and Bruno Walter in 1938, as an alternative to conducting and playing under the Nazi government. After the war other European festivals sprang up in part to reignite cultural programming and to show how all was well: the Prague Spring Festival in 1946, Edinburgh Festival in 1947, and Santander Festival in 1948. To some the festivals became prestige vacations, with the opportunity to hear celebrity performers otherwise out of reach. To others they were the locus of tired re-readings from the main season that demonstrated just how closed the canon had become.

In Boston the practice was to ease gently from the subscription season into the Pops concerts (originally played by the same musicians, minus the principals) and then on to Tanglewood, the Tappan family estate in the mountains outside Lenox, Massachusetts. Koussevitzky's pet project was the school for young musicians there, the Berkshire Music Center, which he established in 1940 and where many of his successors—Bernstein, Ozawa, Mehta, Maazel, Tilson Thomas, Abbado, to name only a few—were apprenticed. In the summer of 1949, a Chicago couple hosted the Goethe Bicentennial Convocation and Music Festival in Aspen, Colorado, promoting Greek ideals of life lived in harmony with nature and music. "Once in a lifetime," read the advertisements, "is such a vacation yours." The Aspen Music Festival welcomes 750 professional-level orchestra students each summer.

Full-time orchestras by their definition have summer homes, often outdoors: Ravinia in Chicago, Robin Hood Dell in Philadelphia, the Hollywood Bowl. The pleasure of picnicking with the symphony orchestra overcomes the disadvantages of crowd size and sudden reverses in the weather. Festivals are indispensable in establishing the connections that build new audiences and lead to the community satisfaction at the heart of every modern mission statement.

Chapter 4
Money

The basic calculus for an early nineteenth-century concert series was rudimentary: take the season's ticket income, subtract the production costs, and divide the result among the musicians. In its simplest form, cash from subscription sales would be placed in a strongbox from which the treasurer would settle accounts as they were presented. After the last concert the contents of the strongbox were distributed equally among the players, adjusted for absence and the occasional penalty for bad behavior.

The old collectives allowed for pay differentials by job title: the conductor might make twice what the musicians did. As the principal players—the leader/concertmaster and the section heads—began to command higher fees, the proportional distribution might be twice as much for the principals, eight times for the conductor. The players themselves did most of the personnel and materiel management, simply for the satisfaction of service. The expenses of an orchestra include costs of the venue—principally heating it and lighting it, as well as staffing it with police, firemen, ushers, porters, and tuners for the low strings and keyboard instruments at concert time—and the upkeep of the instruments and library. For a very long time the overhead was a routine, limited expense, with the majority of the proceeds going directly to the players.

These primitive but workable conditions prevailed into the twentieth century, but since seasons were fully subscribed revenues were fixed, and the central financial question became the demand for increased numbers in the ensemble: woodwinds in threes, a tuba player. The 1920s brought radical changes in the expenditure of leisure time, where sports and the family automobile competed with concert music. Concepts of the orchestral product changed with radio and records. The implicit understanding that orchestras and their conductors belonged in one place but for brief, exceptional periods of leave was abandoned. The orchestra became fully exposed to European-American economic cycles.

But over the long haul, and throughout the world, the most intractable business problem was a direct result of orchestral music's wild popularity: the star system, where a few conductors, concerto soloists, and their managers commanded such astronomical fees for single appearances as to rewrite the underlying principles of the ledger. The 2003–04 payroll for the Los Angeles Philharmonic showed $1.3 million for the conductor, $800,000 for the chief executive, and a base salary for the players of $113,000 rising to $350,000 for the concertmaster. (These were by some distance the highest non-movie arts salaries in the state.) In the 1960s an equally relentless new pressure began to exert itself: the idea, and ideal, that fifty-two-week, full-time employment in a single organization was the orchestra player's rightful entitlement.

By the turn of the twenty-first century most symphony orchestras were worrying themselves along in continuous monetary crisis, even as tectonic shifts elsewhere in the music industry had to be absorbed. As classical music and its chief representative redefine their place in civic culture, the demographic, economic, and scholarly arguments inevitably lead back to the discovery of the 1820s: that the balance sheet follows the philharmonia quotient— how orchestras, their public, their cities, and the music they make resonate with one another.

Patronage

Ticket income alone never paid a living wage to an ordinary orchestra musician. The number of musicians involved in a symphony concert and the length of time it takes to prepare one properly made certain of that. Patrons were always there: the sovereign who would guarantee in advance to meet a deficit, lesser nobility who would pay greatly more for prestige seating, well-connected socialites who enjoyed organizing benefit concerts.

Ancien régime thinking held that it was the responsibility of government ministers to assure that the nation's patrimony was protected. Generous subventions to the old European orchestras, like those to opera houses and theater companies, were common by the late nineteenth century. So was their downside, the imposition of conditions by the funding authorities, usually seeking to glorify local or national art over imports. *Dwight's Journal of Music* reported in 1859 the operating cost of the Dresden State Theatre with its orchestra and subscription concert series to be $200,000, offset by state subvention of $30,000 to $40,000 to the house and another $40,000 to the orchestra. The Berlin Philharmonic survived the years after World War I with a ten-year guaranteed income from the city of 480,000 marks, thus shifting from a private orchestra to a state-sponsored one. The Orchestre de Paris, at its much-heralded debut in 1968, was subventioned by a basket of funds: 50 percent from the nation, 33 percent from the city of Paris, and 17 percent from the council of local governments in the Seine region.

Experiments with government subventions in the United States, ranging from the Federal Music Project (1935–1940) to the present National Endowment for the Arts, failed to provide orchestras with a reliable safety net. Beginning with Theodore Thomas in Chicago, the differential between ticket income and season expense was always met by private and corporate philanthropy. Civic-minded industrial barons with names like Carnegie, Pulitzer, and Heinz, and of course their wives, spent their inherited wealth or the products of their capital enterprise to guarantee that the city they called home had its measure of high art. When one fortune was exhausted, another would present itself, and when the one-party system threatened to fail, boards of trustees were content to take on the operating loss in equal shares. When that responsibility became too onerous for individual board members, the burden of meeting deficits was transferred to subscriber groups, businessmen who knew little of orchestral life, and the public at large. The community appeal—Save Our Symphony—became a way of life. European musicians viewed this with a mix of bemusement and envy.

Central to the American orchestra movement were the women's auxiliary associations often called the Symphony League. "Give me six women, a bag of cookies and a box of tea and you'll have your symphony orchestra," remarked Samuel Rosenbaum, an attorney and board member of the Philadelphia Orchestra. "The leagues create money where none exists," remarked a woman executive. "They invent ticket purchasers and audience members. . . . They have a wondrous abiding faith that somehow the way can be found to do what is needed to serve the orchestra: time after time, city after city, season after season, crisis after crisis."

Women activists were behind the formation of the American Symphony Orchestra League (ASOL), now called the League of American Orchestras, in 1942. Its first executive was Helen M. Thompson, who left her position as manager of the Charleston (West Virginia) Symphony Orchestra to take the job, serving from 1950 to 1970 and then leaving it to become the manager of the New York Philharmonic. The league and its magazine, *Symphony*, have long been the national clearing house for orchestra news and industry-wide initiatives. Among its successful undertakings was to have symphony tickets exempted from the federal luxury tax of 20 percent.

As women joined the workplace, the ladies' auxiliaries declined in number and exposure, but women continue to occupy critical positions in orchestral governance and support. The philanthropists Louise M. Davies, Lillian Disney, and Margrit Mondavi, for instance, continued to sustain interests they had established with their late husbands. Three formidable California venues testify to their zeal.

Managers and empires

Haydn's two seasons in London were produced by J. P. Salomon, who fetched the composer from Vienna, undertook the business arrangements and the risk, and played violin in the concerts, thereby establishing the principle that artist management and concert organization were different threads of the same fabric. Liszt's Paris secretary, Gaetano Belloni, made the advance arrangements for the most peripatetic of all the traveling virtuoso-composer-conductors and in so doing developed many characteristics of the modern press agent. For brazen daring, few adventures can match the contract between P. T. Barnum and the soprano Jenny Lind for an 1850 concert tour of the United States, with orchestra, conductor (Julius Benedict), and an assisting baritone singer. The proffered fee was $1,000 a night for 150 nights, though in the end a renegotiated agreement that addressed the question of residuals yielded her some $250,000 for ninety-three concerts—in modern purchasing power, some $7 million. Barnum netted twice that.

It was widely recognized by this time that the soloists, conductors, and orchestras most in demand required professional management. The patriarch of the profession was Hermann Wolff, whose Concert Direction Hermann Wolff in Berlin, established 1880, became the central clearinghouse for orchestral performance in upper Europe. Engaged to book soloists and conductors for both the Leipzig Gewandhaus Orchestra and the Frankfurt Museumsgesellschaft concerts, he then negotiated the Berlin Philharmonic into existence in 1882 and persuaded to conduct it not only Hans von Bülow in 1887 but also Bülow's successor, the great Arthur Nikisch, in 1895. (Berlin thus took from Leipzig the distinction of having Germany's principal orchestra.) Wolff's connections with the Russian musical establishment were close, and it was he who promoted Tchaikovsky's 1891 visit to the United States for the opening of Carnegie Hall. Wolff's widow, Louise—commonly called Queen Louise of Prussia—carried on the business and essentially administered the Berlin Philharmonic for the rest of her life, recruiting Nikisch's successor, the young Wilhelm Furtwängler, in 1925.

In Paris the impresario Gabriel Astruc, after a string of brilliant successes in his annual Grande Saison de Paris seasons (Caruso, the premiere of *Salome* with Strauss conducting, Diaghilev's Ballets Russes), built the Théâtre des Champs-Elysées and opened it in May 1913 with a paradigmatic blockbuster season, including the legendary first night of *The Rite of Spring*, which ruined him. Thereafter the *bureau de concerts* Marcel de Valmalète, still today a family enterprise, controlled Parisian orchestral planning and the export of such *de luxe* commodities as Ravel and Arthur Rubinstein.

Agents kept the pulse of the market. They knew everybody and served as the profession's news source and crisis management experts. They provided a line of tedious, grimy services that artists were happy to pay to be relieved of. They became indispensable and in turn all powerful.

Arthur Judson, called AJ, a physically imposing giant of the industry, became the czar of American orchestral life as the result of his innate grasp of how big music functioned in and around New York. A violinist *manqué*, he acquired his knowledge of concert life as advertising manager and traveling reviewer for the powerful weekly magazine, *Musical America*. Leopold Stokowski engaged Judson in 1915 to manage the Philadelphia Orchestra, and the following year they together produced Mahler's Symphony of a Thousand in ten sold-out performances including a commute to the Metropolitan Opera House in New York. Stokowski was essentially elevated to overnight stardom, while Concert Management Arthur Judson, Inc., began to dominate orchestral affairs in both cities. Judson became in short succession (and simultaneously) manager of the New York Philharmonic (1922), co-founder with Philadelphia businessman William Paley of the Columbia Broadcasting System in (1927), and principal partner of Columbia Concerts (1930), later Columbia Artists Management Inc., or CAMI. His commission was 20 percent.

Judson's chief competitor was David Sarnoff, the brains behind big music at RCA and NBC. Together these two brilliant minds, and the cartels they established, transformed local orchestral enterprise into international big business. Live concerts, radio (and very soon television), and the sale of ever more seductive phonograph records were purposefully and inextricably linked. The fortunes of the orchestras so privileged—principally those of New York, Boston, Philadelphia, and Chicago—rose astonishingly. As Columbia's Community Concerts and NBC's Civic Concerts, the competitors engaged in bitter combat for municipal audiences in every corner of the nation. *Time* magazine called this "Chain-Store Music" and described "a stooge setup," where "a salesman calls on the local bigwiggery and the clubwomen, cajoles them into a week's fund-raising campaign to put Podunk on the musical map." Flagrant conflicts of interests were inherent in the system: Bruno Zirato, who had come to New York as Caruso's secretary, was simultaneously Judson's assistant at Columbia and manager of the New York Philharmonic.

The modern CAMI, in fact, emerged as a business entity specifically to avoid a federal antitrust investigation against Arthur Judson's enterprises. Indeed, the only serious challenge to CAMI in America came from the Ukrainian immigrant Sol Hurok, whose agency S. Hurok Presents flourished for forty years by delivering the cornerstones of Soviet culture—the Kirov and Moiseyev ballet companies, the great Soviet instrumentalists, Rudolf Nureyev—to American audiences hungry for anything Russian but missiles.

Conductors and soloists were the chief clients of this system, while the orchestra had to bear the brunt of its cost. Judson was succeeded at CAMI in 1961 by Ronald Wilford, whose obsession with a roster of conductors as personal clients—Herbert von Karajan, Seiji Ozawa, James Levine, Claudio Abbado, and Riccardo Muti among his favorites—was sufficient to control orchestral life in the United States and abroad for decades. He reckoned his business creed to be maximizing the wealth of the artists "that interested us," and before he was done conductor and soloist fees amounted to half an orchestra's annual budget. His clients made in one night three or four times what the average orchestral musician made in a year.

Wilford and CAMI are held to be the root cause of the monetary imbalances that came to a head in the 1990s. Yet to the extent that the professional concert managers challenged orchestras to establish advanced business practices, guided the lonely prodigy along the path to celebrity, and found new customers at the nodes of intersection, they did an effective job. It fell to the local orchestra manager to broker the best interests of the orchestra, notably in collective bargaining with the players. Orchestra managers, a small and intriguing coterie, quickly outdistanced players and even conductors as primary spokespersons for "the industry."

Foundations and endowments in the United States

John F. Kennedy and his wife, Jacqueline, had Casals and Copland and Bernstein over to the White House; they wrote affectionate notes to Charles Munch in Boston, gave youth concerts on the White House lawn, and promoted the enabling legislation for the National Endowment for the Arts (NEA) and what became the Kennedy Center. And if the NEA, created by act of Congress in 1965, was never more than minuscule in financial clout (today .05 percent of the federal budget, in the area of $150 million for all the arts—roughly the same amount as the combined budgets of the Boston and New York orchestras), the gesture was nonetheless dramatic. The American symphony orchestra was at its peak.

In July 1966, after studies begun in 1957, the Ford Foundation granted more than $80 million to sixty-one American orchestras, at the time the largest arts grant in history. Trumpeted as "Millions for Music—Music for Millions," the stated mission was "to bring more and better music to more people." Some $59 million was granted directly to orchestra endowments in the form of five-year challenge grants, with the rest distributed in annual cash installments. The foundation reckoned that when the matching was complete, $195 million in new support for American symphony orchestras would have been generated. A significant nationwide growth in orchestra budgets was predicted: 16.8 percent for 1966–67 and ongoing after that.

The twenty-five major orchestras in 1965–66 showed combined expenditures of $31,375,000. On average their contributed income was just short of 25 percent of budget, though two orchestras had more than 50 percent. The orchestral endowment was recognized as critical to the annual funding stream, in the best case covering upwards of 7 percent of annual costs. Government funding, mostly for school concerts, was just short of 5 percent: $2.3 million nationwide in 1965–66. Supporting figures showed a healthy national increase in symphony orchestra attendance between 1962–63 and 1964–65.

The Ford Foundation's specific intent was to stimulate the growth of full-time employment for orchestral musicians, "one of the most underpaid professional groups in American society." While the average salary in the Big Five (Boston, Philadelphia, New York, Chicago, and Cleveland) was $11,600 for 1965–66, the remaining orchestras paid $5,000 or less. Even the Big Five salaries were only marginally higher than those of public school teachers, whose work year was considerably shorter. These were hardly the conditions of prestige employment.

To stem the flow of musicians from the regionals to the Big Five, a central provision of the foundation's scheme was to stimulate annual income for the player far afield "sufficient to enable him to give up a public-school position or other job that now prevents him from attending day-time rehearsals." Other funds were designated to afford extra rehearsal time for expanding the repertoire. The overarching themes were roughly the same as they are today, stressing service to the community (usually expressed in terms of pops concerts and commemorative events like Martin Luther King Day ceremonies) and the education of its young, attention to the demographic shift of audiences toward the suburbs, and the need to partner with local opera, ballet, and choral organizations. Expansion was assumed to be the desired outcome. The "general atmosphere is one of excitement and optimism," crowed the foundation, certain their investment would "substantially affect the musical consciousness of the entire nation."

Constituencies were, for a time, electrified. But even before the conclusion of the grant period a decade later, the weaknesses in the strategy had begun to reveal themselves. Contract bargaining grew hostile as musicians insisted on giant steps toward a dream outcome. The move to daytime rehearsals as local orchestras edged toward full-time employment robbed them of the very college professors and double-threat professionals who had founded their institutions to begin with, and who were already the tightest link between the orchestra and its community. They were replaced by recent graduates disappointed not to have made it higher in the food chain and imagining they would stay in town for just a few months. The Andrew W. Mellon Foundation, after routine grants from 1977 to 1984, suspended its funding of symphony orchestras altogether, having concluded that the environment was unhealthy, the sector's financial performance poor, the labor disputes debilitating. In short, orchestras were no longer worth the investment.

The millennium crisis

Alarms were sounding everywhere by the 1990s. A string of major orchestra failures rocked the profession: Oakland in 1986, Denver in 1989, New Orleans in 1991. Northern California alone lost three important orchestras; there was no professional orchestra left in Florida or Hawaii. Some managed to reorganize, the Colorado Symphony, Louisiana Philharmonic, and Tulsa Symphony, for instance, but the successor orchestras were invariably poorer with much shorter seasons. Infrastructure, including endowments and music libraries, was lost. The civic agony was unbearable and in some cases irreversible: civic leaders tired not only of the struggle but also of the vilification, while the public tired of subscribing to seasons annulled before the end.

Globally things were no better, owing to the apparent collapse of the recording industry. The London essayist Norman Lebrecht dates the death of classical music as July 7, 1990, the occasion of the first Three Tenors concert, Zubin Mehta conducting, in the Roman Baths of Caracalla on the eve of the 1990 World Cup final. His several accounts of excess and addiction in the upper echelons of the music business, CAMI to EMI, are an unrelenting story of power exercised for personal and corporate profit at the expense of art. From his London birds-nest, Lebrecht enumerates and then bemoans consistently destructive behaviors that gathered into widespread bankruptcy both fiscal and moral.

In 1999 the Mellon Foundation, seeking to understand these upheavals, established The Orchestra Forum, a panel of orchestra managers, players, and observers called to examine the field and apply solutions over a ten-year period. The program officer, Catherine Wichterman, presented a breathtaking list of figures: an American establishment consisting of 1,200 professional orchestras with $1 billion in revenue, a sturdy component—after art museums perhaps the sturdiest—of the American arts market. Only a small percentage of these orchestras (13 percent) had large budgets, and only seventeen had fifty-two-week seasons and budgets over $10 million. There were 78,000 professional orchestral musicians in the country and 11,000 staff, giving 27,000 concerts in a year's time to 32 million ticket-holders. But the catalog of woes was thick and sharply focused on flawed leadership, especially absentee conductors and the functional collapse of the management–trustee–musician triangle. Job satisfaction among the musicians ranked behind that of flight attendants and prison guards.

The Orchestra Forum sought to apply modern economic tools and analytical systems to the problem at hand in an effort to answer whether the obvious escalation in economic woes was "cyclical," reflecting business cycles, where good times and bad times theoretically balance out over time, or "structural" and therefore permanent. Already in 1966, the Princeton economists William J. Baumol and William G. Bowen (soon to be president of Princeton, then of the Mellon) proposed in *Performing Arts: The Economic Dilemma* that the industry falls in a category where "productivity" can never increase, thereby undercutting ordinary standards of business.

Robert J. Flanagan, a Stanford economist commissioned by the Mellon Foundation, demonstrated in 2007 that the "performance income gap," that is, the margin between the expense of live performance (salaries) and the performance revenue (ticket sales) was consistently increasing. That was not especially surprising— in fact, everybody knew it already—but the degree of the trend was shocking: over the preceding seventeen years, performance expense had grown three times faster than performance revenue.

For the second five years of the study period, 2003–08, an Elephant Task Force, so-called to suggest the preservationist movement, scrutinized the issues from every angle it could control. It asked the fundamental questions of whether the American orchestra was any longer capable of functioning,

The Orchestra

and (more interestingly) whether it was the right vehicle "to preserve and advance classical music tradition." It was a vexed and vexing process, characterized by a lack of audited data from enough constituents and by the difficulty of suspending long-held suspicions as to where the blame lay. "No one found it comforting." In the end, the recommendations focused on ways to renegotiate the original philharmonic ideal: reconnecting with the community, on the one hand, and keeping at the front end of the intellectual concerns of art music on the other.

Monetary crisis at the symphony orchestra hardly went away as governments and donors wrestled to bring their own budgets under control. In April 2011 the Philadelphia Orchestra became the first of the Big Five orchestras to file for bankruptcy, struggling to close a budget gap in the area of $10 million, presumably with pay cuts and layoffs. In New York, where the value of the Philharmonic's once comfortable endowment lost more than $40 million during the recession that began in late 2007, there was a $4.5 million deficit for 2009–10.

The situation in Detroit, a "Rust Belt" city with structural problems considerably greater than how to maintain a symphony orchestra, was closely watched. Detroit Symphony musicians were asked to take a 23 percent cut in their base pay of $104,6500, refused it, and went on strike in October 2010. A final offer for a contract was rejected in February 2011, and the 2010–11 season was suspended.

A settlement reached in Detroit a few days before the Philadelphia bankruptcy left the musicians with a base salary of roughly $79,000 for a thirty-six-week season, with a possibility of further stipends for a voluntarily "educational and community outreach component"—a net loss in compensation of about 25 percent. The rhetoric had of course emphasized the clash between celebrity salaries ($500,000 for the CEO; something on the order of $1 million for the conductor, both of whom continued to earn their salaries during the interruptions) and working musicians with

4. Musicians of the Detroit Symphony Orchestra picket outside Orchestra Hall, October 2010.

similar training and ability. There was widespread solidarity from working musicians across the country, but widespread incredulity from bystanders as to musician demands in a devastated economy. Leonard Slatkin, the conductor, kept his own counsel and took no sides, reasoning as conductors usually do that in the end he would have to be the fence-mender.

There was some good news nationwide: with non-performance income (private gifts, grants, and the like) counted in, a "gentle trend toward surplus" might be imagined. The Los Angeles Philharmonic was in a four-year contract that would see a 17 percent raise to nearly $149,000 in base pay by 2012. This was in part the work of a new superstar of orchestra affairs, Deborah Borda, the LA Phil's chief executive officer. Armed with a strong education (Bennington College and the Royal College of Music in London) and serious orchestral experience, Borda had arrived at the New York Philharmonic, which was widely agreed to be ailing artistically and financially, living only on its endowment of $100 million, established by Joseph Pulitzer, for its 150th anniversary in 1992, and was expected to shock an orchestra into what she later called "close to a decade of robust artistic and financial health." Among her innovations were the successful rush-hour concerts on weeknights at 6:45, lasting for just over an hour and theoretically allowing commuters simply to take a later train home. Called to the Los Angeles Philharmonic at the start of the new millennium, Borda oversaw the opening of the new Disney Hall and the transition of conductors from Esa-Pekka Salonen to Gustavo Dudamel. Her great success in bringing the musicians, conductor, public, and venue into unparalleled resonance has made that orchestra the success story of the epoch.

The determination to survive thus has some models to emulate. To a provocative report presented by the arts consultant Thomas Wolf before the American Symphony Orchestra League in 1992 ("The industry as a whole appears to be in the worst financial shape it has ever been in"; "How viable is the full-time 90- to 100-piece orchestra"?), the responses were apt and rich with good thinking from brilliant leaders: Borda, then still in New York, Peter Pastreich of the San Francisco Symphony, and John McClaugherty of the West Virginia Symphony Orchestra. As to viability and size, Pastreich responded that "it's been pretty viable for well over a century, but 120 to 140 musicians *would* be better," then went on to defend the strengths of an institution that, contrary to Wolf's seeming assertion, had "never been upper-class," and that remained "the most totally equal opportunity in America: the best paying position that a person of color, a gay or lesbian, or a woman can get purely on the bases of experience and performance, without ever having to submit a letter of recommendation or undergo a personal interview." While acknowledging that orchestras cannot spend more than they take in, he concluded that "the situation is critical, not serious, and music will survive."

Chapter 5
Conductors

The contemporary conductor is the central paradox of orchestra affairs: the personification of the ensemble, but likely as not to be out of town. His or her artistic duty is singular in purpose, to plan and lead the concerts, but the common expectation is that the conductor will teach young and old alike, serve as tradition's guardian and high priest, cultivate philanthropy, and exude charisma as spokesperson for the merits of high art.

Conductors do not ordinarily reach the podium without having demonstrated prodigious gifts and a pronounced work ethic. They were seasoned instrumentalists before they began conducting, and in subsequent apprenticeships developed acute powers of hearing and ear-eye-body rapport. At the keyboard they reduce dozens of lines to the work of two hands. Reading an orchestral score demands a unique kind of mental agility: the love scene from Berlioz's *Roméo et Juliette* has four horn parts, each pitched in a different key and thus needing to be transposed on the fly, and a recent Brian Ferneyhough orchestral score is a meter square with individual staves for every player in a hundred-piece orchestra. The listening is unusual, too, since the conductor simultaneously dictates what is supposed to happen while fine-tuning what just occurred. The repertoire is huge and increases every year, and the conductor must be capable of advancing it.

The martinet, typically imported from central Europe, of amusing accent and unseemly temper, has largely died out, and with him the willingness of musicians and trustees to delegate to the conductor unlimited power to hire and fire. Disappearing, too, is the concentration of wealth and prestige in the hands of a half-dozen or fewer megastars like Herbert von Karajan and Leonard Bernstein. Conductors in the new century seem closer to earth.

Chapelmaster and composer-conductor

The profession of conducting emerged with the philharmonic society. Chapelmasters like Bach and Handel saw to the organization and execution of every detail of performance at their establishments and composed much of the music themselves. The Brandenburg concertos were doubtless led by Bach from a keyboard, much as the Mozart piano concertos assumed the composer at the piano for the solo part. Haydn conducted from the keyboard or with his violin and bow in hand: at the end of the "Farewell" Symphony No. 45, the two violinists left onstage were Haydn and his concertmaster, Luigi Tomasini. François-Antoine Habeneck, who introduced Beethoven to the French, conducted with his violin bow from a first violin part.

Even before Beethoven's Ninth, it was growingly clear that the chief executive needed eyes and hands—and brain—free if there were to be adequate control of difficult music for ever larger forces. The pioneers of the profession—Louis Spohr, Berlioz, Mendelssohn—abandoned any intent to play along, standing before the players and leading with a baton in the right hand. (Another pioneer, Carl Maria von Weber, conducted with a roll of paper in his right hand.) Berlioz got into the profession owing to disaffection with how the local conductors played his works, but he went on to become the leading exponent of the Beethoven symphonies. Mendelssohn, whose official title in Leipzig was Gewandhaus-kapellmeister, oversaw the epicenter of the German orchestral establishment. Among his lasting accomplishments was restoring the St. Matthew Passion of Bach to the central repertoire and playing Schubert's symphonies as they were retrieved from oblivion.

The composer-conductors scheduled their lives around their concert responsibilities, composing off season. They traveled widely to lead their concerts, Berlioz and Wagner once appearing simultaneously in London with rival philharmonic societies. (Berlioz complained that hearing Wagner conduct was like "dancing for an hour on slack wire.") Mahler retreated each summer from staggering administrative responsibilities with the Vienna Opera and Philharmonic to a tiny "composing hut" by his villa in the mountains—then would return willingly to the hurly-burly each fall. Richard Strauss was also a virtuoso conductor, often compared to or contrasted with Mahler, as for example at a Strasbourg festival performance in May 1905, when Strauss conducted his *Sinfonia domestica* and Mahler his Fifth Symphony

5. Carl Maria von Weber conducts a concert at Covent Garden, London, 1826. He faces the orchestra (in the pit) and audience, with the singers behind him.

and Beethoven's Ninth. The composer-conductors wrote about their new profession. Berlioz added a chapter on conducting to his famous *Treatise on Orchestration*, diagramming baton patterns still in common use. Among Wagner's hundreds of turgid pages on conducting is a compelling essay on how a conductor might think about Beethoven's Ninth.

Most twentieth-century conductors dabbled in composition, to little lasting effect. Wrestling with the balance was the central issue of Leonard Bernstein's artistry; Esa-Pekka Salonen said he became a conductor because he was bored with composition. The trend toward the specialist conductor had been set long before by Hans von Bülow, as a result of the technical demands incumbent on conducting Wagner's operas. Von Bülow was the soloist in the premiere of the Tchaikovsky Piano Concerto (Boston, 1875), then went on to provide the environment, with the court orchestra in Meiningen, where Brahms perfected his symphonic technique and where Richard Strauss gained his first conducting experience. He rehearsed and conducted from memory, and occasionally had the

6. Gustav Mahler conducts Beethoven's Ninth Symphony in Strasbourg, May 22, 1905.

orchestra do the same. His orchestra played standing up, in the old Gewandhaus tradition.

Score, baton, podium

The profession of conducting, as developed after Beethoven, had those three defining attributes. Use of the full score by the conductor made it possible to proceed without the composer present and was essential for reference during rehearsals; the concept of strict fidelity to the score soon replaces notions of individual players free to improvise on the lines before them. The baton took multiple forms, from the thin switch seen already in the hands of singing teachers portrayed in medieval manuscript illuminations to field-marshal batons grasped about the middle. Its primary purpose, and that of the podium, was to make the conductor's gestures clear from increasing distances. This was especially important for the growing number of works with large chorus, sometimes also controlled by assistant conductors and even by the large "electric metronome" favored for a time in nineteenth-century Paris.

Assisting conductors for offstage and satellite ensembles have in large measure been replaced by video feeds from the podium. They remain essential in exceptional circumstances: Charles Ives, for instance, calls briefly in his Fourth Symphony for two conductors to shape essentially rival groups. (Excerpts from a remarkable performance can be seen on YouTube, where Leopold Stokowski and the young José Serebrier lead the American Symphony Orchestra in Carnegie Hall, April 1965, in the "world premiere" of a work some fifty years old.) Some chamber orchestras play without a stand-alone conductor, with the concertmaster-leader in charge; and in the old Soviet Union, as a political statement, an orchestra called Persimfans (from the Russian for "First Conductorless Symphony Ensemble Orchestra") undertook the symphonic repertoire, without particular success (1922–32).

A conductor's gestures come from tradition and training at the academy, personalized during a career of finding moves that result in desired effect. How to convey tempo and point of attack or release is the critical matter, but so too is prompting recall of what has been rehearsed and shaping the progress of a work over the course of its full duration. Much of the rest is inconsequential. Conducting "from memory," for instance, is no particular measure of ability. One conducts without score for a variety of legitimate reasons, including myopia; having the score at hand is reassuring in some circumstances and essential in others, never a reason for a negative judgment. The German conductor Hans Knappertsbusch famously remarked "Of course I use a score. I can read music."

Several leading conductors, including Valery Gergiev, following the practice of Stokowski, conduct without a baton, finding the hands alone to be more expressive. Some of the most interesting conductors use the baton on-and-off or let it come to rest for a time in the left hand. Carlos Kleiber would abandon right-hand patterns to concentrate on nuance with his left. Mendelssohn sometimes stopped conducting altogether, thinking "this will go very well without me."

The maestro

Hans von Bülow's protégé Arthur Nikisch established the maestro paradigm, characterized not so much by celebrity behavior as by encyclopedic knowledge of the repertoire and ability to galvanize players and then the public during the live concert. Simultaneously conductor of the Leipzig and Berlin orchestras, he brought both to international prominence through indefatigable touring and some of the earliest symphonic recordings (for example, Beethoven's Fifth with the Berlin Philharmonic, 1913). He himself traveled the world, serving briefly as resident conductor of the Boston Symphony Orchestra and repeatedly as invited guest on podiums from London to Moscow and St. Petersburg, and doing much to establish Tchaikovsky's symphonies in the canon.

Modern conducting descends from, or reacts to, the two giants of the trade who succeeded Nikisch, Arturo Toscanini and Wilhelm Furtwängler. But two more different approaches and personalities it is difficult to imagine. Toscanini preached fidelity to the score and disciplined technique, then with legendary tantrums excoriated his players into terrified but powerful responses that had little to do with either fidelity or discipline. Furtwängler lacked refinement of gesture but was able to reshape even the warhorses of the Austro-German repertoire into readings that felt new and compelling. Furtwängler's career was largely over after World War II, as his was the probably unwilling orchestral face of the German supremacists—just as Toscanini, heroically anti-Fascist, reached the peak of his celebrity with the NBC Symphony Orchestra from 1937 to 1954. The influence of their disciples and recorded artifacts on orchestral values in the second half of the twentieth century is all pervasive. For instance Charles Munch, who had been Furtwängler's concertmaster in Leipzig, brought his violin to sit in on Toscanini's rehearsals in Paris and spoke often afterward on how formative these two experiences had been to his own approach.

They are a colorful bunch, the *maestri*, long on ego and power, and often as not consumed in doubt as they confront frightening scores and insatiable audience demands. There are the peacocks like Mitropoulos and his disciple Leonard Bernstein, given to opera cloaks and top hats: Bernstein wore Koussevitzky's cufflinks and ceremoniously kissed them before he took stage. Stokowski, born and raised in London, affected a vague pan-European accent and enjoyed, as his taxi passed Big Ben, asking companions: "Tell me. What is big clock?" Thomas Beecham, known everywhere as Sir Thomas, was of a magnificent but amusing arrogance. When asked in 1948 whether it was a privilege to come to the Edinburgh Festival, he responded: "Good God, no! It is an honour and a privilege to the Festival for me to come here." When asked what he thought of the 1956 visit of the Boston Symphony to Edinburgh, he replied "I never go to concerts other than my own. I find my own are unpleasant enough without listening to others, which I am sure are worse."

The Viennese conductor Carlos Kleiber, named in a 2011 poll of a hundred professional conductors the greatest "of all time," led a mere ninety-six concerts in his career, achieving his reputation in part by *not* conducting, then commanding magnificent sums and unprecedented hours of rehearsal time to come out of hiding. One can understand his reluctance: he was the son of the great conductor Erich Kleiber, who had formally opposed his career choice, and was prone to feeling incapable of describing what he wanted to the musicians. And one can understand the vote: consider the 1986 videos of the Bavarian State Orchestra, touring in Japan. In a *Fledermaus* overture offered as an encore, the essence of great conducting is captured, where concept, subtlety of detail, and gestural perfection yield a perfect melding of composition, conductor, and players. Never mind that the pastiche overture was not meant to be consequential.

The *maestri* imported to the United States from Europe—Serge Koussevitzky to Boston, Eugene Ormandy to Philadelphia, George Szell to Cleveland, Dimitri Mitropoulos to New York, later Georg Solti to Chicago—conditioned Americans to the style. Szell, a man of musical gifts often described as the equal of Mozart's, was the ultimate autocrat, who by virtue of consummate intelligence and endless drill honed the provincial ensemble he inherited in 1946 into what was by the 1960s widely regarded as the world's best orchestra. Many of the Columbia Masterworks stereo recordings of Szell and the Cleveland remain definitive, none more so than the Dvořák symphonies and Slavonic Dances. His protégés, including James Levine and Leon Fleischer, excelled. Even those who found his performances sterile in their perfection were impressed with the clarity of the message. His musicians feared him but played well for him, they said, out of respect. By contrast, when Koussevitzky was succeeded by Munch in Boston, a musician remarked "Now we can play without ulcers."

Like Szell, the conductors of the middle third of the twentieth century established close ties with the societies that had adopted them. The resident conductor was expected for the majority of the concerts in a season, lasting variously between eighteen and thirty pairs, and usually was discouraged or even enjoined from appearing with other orchestras except during vacation periods. (The 2010 contract for Yannick Nézet-Séguin in Philadelphia, by contrast, called for him to be in residence a half season by his third year.) *Maestri* whetted public interest in repertoire and soloists and young conductors, and planted the desire for modern or modernized venues of unassailable acoustic. With limited opportunity to hear other conductors at work, they nourished highly individualized notions of the orchestral ideal. One can recognize the Philadelphia or Cleveland or Vienna "sound" from those years within a few bars.

A true dictator of the baton was Yevgeny Mravinsky, conductor of the Leningrad / St. Petersburg Philharmonic from 1938 to 1988. His authority over his players was complete. They could be summoned at any time and kept at rehearsal as long as he willed. The videos show him working details—the first two bars of a Brahms movement—for quarter-hours at a stretch. (Szell did this too, demanding rehearsals of a few bars of the Mozart G-Minor Symphony from his well-seasoned orchestra even during a tour.) Naturally reclusive in personality, aloof, Mravinsky was catapulted to fame by the first performance of Shostakovich's Fifth Symphony, at the time the most nuanced meeting of music and governmental ideals in history. Mravinsky's technique resulted in a particular Leningrad sound, extreme in its precision, rich with string sonority, awash in brass vibrato, that elevated the Leningrad orchestra to the top of the trade. The corpus of Russian works from Tchaikovsky to Prokofiev and Shostakovich had no more authentic exponents. The result, there in the majestic hall built for nobles seeking their pleasure, was not only acoustically but also visually and in important ways politically sensational: the niches crowded with listeners, while the diminutive maestro with tiny gestures, often without a baton, seemed to yield centrality of place to his players and the composer.

Music director

When trans-Atlantic air travel became common, the season-long conductor residency became a thing of the past. Conductors traveled from orchestra to orchestra and hall to hall and concluded lucrative deals with the big record companies. Practices that characterized one conductor-orchestra pair from any other faded away. And in the philharmonic societies a new hierarchy necessarily emerged where daily custody of the orchestra increasingly fell to the general manager, while the "music director" shaped the forthcoming seasons but conducted only some of the concerts. (One title currently in vogue, "Music Director and Principal Conductor," is both aggrandizing and redundant.) The remaining dates were distributed to guests and the orchestra's associate conductors, with favored ones given titles like "principal guest conductor." The previous conductor, or "conductor laureate" would usually be welcomed back.

Even with a strong manager, the music director's daily life is long on administrative tasks and hours in the conference room. To follow Mahler through a week of activity in Vienna during concert season is to wonder where he found the time to think about the music he would conduct that night or the stamina to go on. Deployment of the orchestra, from its layout onstage to the number of players called for each work, is primarily the music director's decision. (The vogue for what is now called "European seating," with first and second violins placed antiphonally, is only "authentic" for some portions of the repertoire; what ultimately matters is that blend and spatial envelope make sense.) Individual conductors vary in their approaches to the musical texts. Wagner and Mahler argued for large-scale modernizing of Beethoven's orchestration, and Szell routinely tweaked his Beethoven with full chromatic horn parts. Cuts were once common. Those kinds of traditions now travel with the conductor, where formerly they were a function of the local orchestra's identity.

What happens in orchestra rehearsals, where the bulk of the conductor's hard work is done, is mostly hidden from the public, but the process began to be commonly understood with a 1995 television documentary titled *The Art of Conducting*, subsequently released on videotape and DVD. Many dozens of hours of the superstars Leonard Bernstein and Herbert von Karajan at work were put to tape, perhaps most tellingly in footage documenting the 1985 recording of *West Side Story* with Kiri Te Kanawa and José Carreras. Video clips available on the Internet show fine conductors—Carlos Kleiber, Sergiu Celebidache, Charles Munch, Daniel Barenboim—at work with their orchestras. The ticking clock is their common enemy: the performers have time to stop and consider only representative questions of detail in any one rehearsal. The rest of it comes together as it goes, the result of accumulated styles acquired over the long haul.

Where there are happy marriages of conductors with their players and publics, the philharmonic ideal is achieved. Where the match is wrong to begin with, or soon goes sour, the harm is thoroughgoing. The pistol packing Arthur Rodzinski was bad for New York, then bad for Chicago, and at length retreated into what was by then obvious mental illness. Christoph Eschenbach is admired in Paris but was often embattled in Philadelphia. The unlikely choice of James Levine to succeed Seiji Ozawa in Boston was, while it lasted, a fine match. Despite a lifetime spent largely at the Metropolitan Opera in New York, and with ongoing health challenges, Levine was able to rekindle a fire in Boston that had gone cool as Ozawa and the Bostonians tired of each other: Levine was sometimes cheered with the kind of ecstasy otherwise reserved in Boston for baseball players. Claudio Abbado and Simon Rattle, both outsiders, found good homes in Berlin. The great career-long partnerships have included Colin Davis and the London

Symphony Orchestra, Bernard Haitink and the Concertgebouw, and Zubin Mehta and the Israel Philharmonic.

The young Daniel Barenboim was brilliantly matched with the Orchestre de Paris, then summarily dismissed in a 1989 dispute over the direction, programming, and subsidies for the new Opéra Bastille in Paris, a French bicentennial project of the Mitterand administration. Barenboim was said to have demanded a salary on the order of $1.1 million, incurring the wrath of the reigning arts patron Pierre Bergé. Leaving Paris was good for Barenboim, who went on to a fine tenure as ninth musical director of the Chicago Symphony (1991, succeeding Solti) and at the Berlin Staatsoper, accruing a significant profile in international affairs.

California-born Michael Tilson Thomas clicked in San Francisco from his appointment in 1995. With notable readings of the music of Charles Ives, then with cycles of Mahler and Stravinsky, the San Francisco Symphony became, again, something not to miss. In Los Angeles, similarly, the young Finnish composer-conductor Esa-Pekka Salonen captivated a city for nearly two decades, 1989–2009, working comfortably alongside Ernest Fleischmann to improve the orchestral circumstance and build and occupy the new Disney Hall. He also spotted his successor, Gustavo Dudamel, at a 2004 conducting competition. On Salonen's watch, "flush with money, free of contract disputes, playing to near-capacity audiences, capitalizing on new technologies, the L.A. Phil became that rare creature, a happy orchestra."

Subtly but surely, meanwhile, the pool of young conductors diversified. The process had begun in the mid-twentieth century and later, with such pivotal figures as Dean Dixon and his students Denis de Coteau and James De Priest. Dixon traced the stages of his career by how he was described in the press: first as a Negro conductor, then as an American conductor, and finally simply as conductor. Women conductors followed in the footsteps of the illustrious Nadia Boulanger, one of the great teachers in the history of music. She was the first woman to take the podium of the leading orchestras, premiering, for instance, Stravinsky's "Dumbarton Oaks" Concerto in 1938. Of the many women conductors attracting attention today, the ranking two are JoAnn Falletta at the venerable Buffalo Philharmonic and Marin Alsop at the Baltimore Symphony. The Chinese American conductor Xian Zhang enjoyed a warm relationship with the New York Philharmonic from 2002 and became its associate conductor in 2005; in 2009 she was appointed music director of the Milan Symphony Orchestra.

England, meanwhile, had witnessed the formidable success of Jane Glover and Sian Edwards beginning in the 1980s, especially on the opera podium. They have a clear successor, at the opera house, in Julia Jones. But in the London concert halls, a woman on the podium is still rare. "There are still too few female conductors in charge of orchestras (apart from Jane Glover at the Royal Academy of Music)," complained Tom Service of the *Guardian* in 2010: "there are no women currently in posts high up the orchestral or operatic hierarchy anywhere in Britain."

The maestro myth

In 1991 the industry's sharp-tongued tattletale, Norman Lebrecht, published *The Maestro Myth: Great Conductors in Pursuit of Power*, a polemic on the corruption of a profession less interested in music than personal stardom and wealth. His principal targets were Herbert von Karajan, the barons of the recording industry, and above all Ronald Wilford and Columbia Artist Management, Inc. His disparagement was thoroughgoing, drawing into its sights Wilford's clients Abbado, Barenboim, Davis, and Ozawa, among the hundred or so conductors in CAMI's stable by that time. A good dozen published diatribes have followed along the same lines, and now Lebrecht has a sturdy entry into the blogosphere, Slipped Disc.

Certainly Lebrecht had a point: that conductor stardom and jaw-dropping fees drove one after another orchestra to the point of bankruptcy. Yet despite his pronouncement of the "shameful death" of classical music in the title of a later book, orchestras and conductors were anything but dead. What was obvious was how absurd the maestro phenomenon could be.

Another debunking was that of Joseph Horowitz in *Understanding Toscanini: A Social History of American Concerto Life* (1994), who explained the Toscanini cult as the end result of corporate marketing that purposefully delivered American middle-class audiences a decayed body of old masterpieces by marketing them as "the world's greatest" and "the legendary." Close scrutiny of a promotional film of Toscanini conducting the NBC Symphony in what was supposed to be a patriot-rousing wartime performance of the overture to Verdi's *La Forza del destino* shows what Horowitz was talking about: Toscanini is impetuous to the point of sloughing time from the measures and rendering the violin passagework in the violins unintelligible. Fondly recalled chapters of the orchestra's past are sometimes like that.

Why they matter

In the end a conductor's task is to animate: to bring to life in the present. Conductors shape the music to its moment: to the venue, the players, the listeners, the circumstances of the day. Where conducting is simply an organizational matter, the conductor serving as traffic control officer, it is not a very interesting one. But when the conductor is able to broker meetings of the mind in the service of art, the music becomes invigorated. Good conducting allows beauty to emerge from others; controls excess and finds shape, weight, and substance; resolves problems built into the composition. It finds a way to make the tenth performance as artful as the first. It leaves the trials and tribulations of the day—for every player has a private life—elsewhere. The moment these things are found, the spell is palpable, expressed by the unanimity of purpose onstage and the raptness of attention in the house.

As the second decade of the twenty-first century got under way, the names on every lip were Gustavo Dudamel, in Los Angeles since 2009; Alan Gilbert, in New York since the same year; and, older and presumably wiser, Simon Rattle, whose 2002 election to the podium in Berlin followed his meteoric rise from conservatory and university to the Birmingham Symphony Orchestra (from 1980, when he was twenty-five, to 1998). Rattle survived a no-confidence vote from his musicians in 2008, partly over his intention of playing Karlheinz Stockhausen's massive *Gruppen* in a hangar at the Tempelhof airport, and instead saw his appointment extended until 2018. (Stockhausen, who characterized the attack on the World Trade Center as "the biggest work of art there has ever been," had died in 2007, and the airport, being decommissioned, had figured prominently in World War II and the postwar division of the city.) The still-boyish Rattle maintains his aplomb in a world far from Oxford and Birmingham, chatting amiably from the stage in preconcert videos, said to have his eye on an American engagement—the embodiment, perhaps, of modern Europe.

The conductors who succeeded Leonard Bernstein in New York— Pierre Boulez, Zubin Mehta, Kurt Masur, Lorin Maazel—seemed, especially the last three, peas in a pod: senior imports with a focus on the standard repertoire and a penchant for living elsewhere. Gilbert is by contrast home grown and New Age: multiethnic, Harvard educated, inclined to live in town. Impeccable of technique and unfailingly courteous, he conducts in the grand manner so long favored in New York. Dudamel, of toothy grin and wacky hair and much the youngest of the lot, takes his constituents by storm: the youth orchestras of El Sistema in his native Venezuela, audiences of the Gothenburg Symphony Orchestra in Sweden, where he continues to be chief conductor, the crowd at the Hollywood Bowl. His theme concerts have included a Tchaikovsky-and-Shakespeare program, and in May and June 2011 a series called Brahms Unbound, in which a central work of Brahms is paired with a like-minded new work: the Brahms

Requiem, for instance, with Steven Mackey's *Beautiful Passing* (2008), a reflection on the death of the composer's mother.

None of the three is, so far, regarded as long on personal stamp to the familiar repertoire. Nor is that any longer the true measure of a conductor's art, when the predominant questions are about so many other corners of the orchestral experience. Conducting, today, is primarily about pumping lifeblood into the philharmonic. When conductors are present, fit, rested, and thinking clearly, we understand why they matter.

Chapter 6
Repertoire

Mozart's sudden abandonment of the piano concerto in order to compose the three great end-of-career symphonies of 1788 (E-flat Major, G Minor, and C Major "Jupiter," K. 543, 550, and 551) is a good example of a repertoire in mutation. European audiences who had supped for decades on Haydn and then Mozart and Beethoven were turning by the 1830s and '40s to Mendelssohn to satisfy their hunger for novelty. Parisians never cared much for Brahms symphonies but devoured orchestral excerpts from the Wagner operas. And if music by dead patriarchs gradually overwhelmed concert programs, still there was nothing quite like a first performance of Debussy to get the blood circulating, or the appearance of Mahler or Ravel or Stravinsky to conduct a new work.

The orchestral repertoire necessarily pivots around Beethoven and Brahms, since the orchestra itself is defined by their work and, conversely, their work in terms of its pursuit of the symphonic ideal. Before Beethoven there is classicism; after Brahms comes the collapse of everything, sonata form and conventional harmonic systems included, and the rebuilding of "classical" music in modernist terms. Brahms, looking Janus-headed on the riches of the past and the puzzles of the future, often seems the ultimate orchestral composer.

But in most places and most eras the repertoire is always shifting, led by conductor enthusiasm, audience demand, academic scholarship—and, still, the individual quests of living composers. Berlioz began to be commonly accepted as a great composer only in the 1950s and '60s, about the same time as the reawakening of interest in Haydn's greatness and in what came to be called Baroque favorites. The rage for Rachmaninov was born in the United States, nourished above all by the Philadelphia Orchestra and its conductors and public. The Mahler symphonies, as championed by Mengelberg in Amsterdam and Bernstein in New York, succeeded those of Brahms and Tchaikovsky as the benchmark for conductor accomplishment. (After New York, Bernstein established the Mahler corpus with the Vienna Philharmonic, who at first needed convincing.) Ferde Grofé's *Grand Canyon Suite* (1931), popularized by Toscanini and the NBC Symphony in a recording of 1932, became a favorite in the rush to prove an American style. Its popular appeal rested on the imagery of burro hooves in "On the Trail," and a bray thrown in for good measure. And, too, because of the Philip Morris cigarette commercials that used it to introduce each episode of *I Love Lucy*.

In part because narrative lies at the heart of Romantic thinking and in part for the simple reason that symphonies after Beethoven were long, composers began to explain their intent with movement titles, as in Liszt's *Faust* Symphony, and with stories in the printed program, as in the *Symphonie fantastique*. Storytelling work dominates the repertoire as the 1800s become the 1900s, not merely familiar tales like *The Sorcerer's Apprentice* and *Till Eulenspiegel's Merry Pranks* but the presumably hidden ones of the "New World" Symphony and Tchaikovsky's *Pathétique*. What is sometimes held to be a fundamental shift of the prevailing concert repertoire from "absolute" to "program" music is not that cut and dried, since both approaches were to be heard on nearly every program. Still, it is true that as modernism dawned in the concert hall, listeners would routinely supply programmatic narratives to works that had none, and they came to count on program and

liner notes or preconcert commentary to demystify all but the most
familiar repertoire.

Programming

Confecting the programs, both the individual concerts and across
an orchestral season, is a balancing act played out three or four
years in advance of when the performance actually happens.
The exercise attempts to plot satisfying degrees of celebrity and
familiarity on the one hand, and space to explore on the other.
Agents broker the calendars of soloists and guest conductors;
seasons are equally determined by such factors as when the chorus
can be available and what the rival events in town might be. Every
concert has to draw and retain the attention of the paying guests,
but it must also have intrinsic intellectual merit. The overall season
needs a natural rhythm of its own, though this is less significant a
matter now that full-season subscribers are much less common.

The formulaic orchestral program—a "curtain-raising" overture,
the concerto, intermission, and then the symphony—was never
more than a template, and over time the place of honor has
migrated from the beginning of the concert to the end. (A similar
shift in priorities informs the genre itself, as the front-loaded
symphonies of Beethoven and his predecessors yield their weight
to the finales of the Ninth, and the works of Brahms, Tchaikovsky,
and Mahler.) At the height of his stardom, the pianist Vladimir
Horowitz would play only at the close of a concert. From the
earliest decades of subscription seasons, in fact, public affection
for the concerto and its soloist threatened to overcome all the other
programming interests, as orchestras sought to deliver such first-
level talent as Clara Schumann playing her husband's concerto,
the Norwegian violinist Ole Bull, or the German-American cello
virtuoso Victor Herbert.

Among the pitfalls of programming are concerts that exceed the
attention span or draw away from the featured work (the Verdi

Requiem preceded by the orchestrated Verdi string quartet) or those that look more interesting on paper than they can be in real life (the Vivaldi "Seasons" concertos played front to back). Single-composer concerts, all-Brahms or all-Wagner, succeed only when they manage to focus the mind on questions of growth or interconnection; otherwise an apt but challenging pairing, say Wagner and Fauré, is more likely to seem distinctive. Orchestral repertoire is subject to vogues, for instance the enthusiasm for Astor Piazzolla and Silvestre Revueltas that broke out in the late 1990s, which require music directors to walk the fine line between recognizing the fad and pandering to it.

Seasons begin and end with grand events usually involving large forces, as in Mahler's "Resurrection" Symphony No. 2 or Carl Orff's *Carmina burana*. Many communities have long-established holiday traditions. The Easter weekend *concert spirituel* in Paris was a contemplative church or churchlike concert and, before that the name given to the season of orchestra concerts that took place during Lent, when the theaters were closed. The Neujahrskonzert of the Vienna Philharmonic every New Year's morning wends a predictable course through music of the Strausses and other Viennese masters of good feeling, broadcast to 50 million people across the world. Pops and Proms repertoire allows shelves of pleasing material into the concert hall: orchestral excerpts drawn from works for the stage, for example, like the Richard Rodgers *Carousel* waltz and Offenbach's *Gaîté parisienne*.

Programming for national tours is nuanced by the need for an orchestra to travel with both its "signature" works and its more contemporary claims to importance, while a sizable proportion of the consumers would just as soon hear another Tchaikovsky Fourth. What to play to foreign audiences is even more nuanced. Everyone wants to hear the Russian orchestras play Russian music; the Berliners, Richard Strauss; the Viennese, Mozart and Schubert and Brahms. But what should Americans play abroad? The Boston Symphony took works of Samuel Barber, Aaron

Copland, Walter Piston, Norman dello Joio, Easley Blackwood, and Leon Kirchner—all closely associated with the orchestra—to Japan in 1960, and critics wondered why a Japanese composer failed to figure on the program. The Philadelphians played Sibelius in Finland and, as ping-pong diplomats, the collective-produced *Yellow River Concerto* in Maoist China in 1973, with pianist-composer Yin Chengzong.

Repertoire trends

What is generally called the canonization of the repertoire was primarily the work of symphony orchestras and their audiences. The nature of the employment of eighteenth-century composers was such that the majority of their work was ephemeral. The inherent nature of programming a concert series, on the other hand, elevated relatively few composers and their works to public attention. These were the ones deemed worthy of repeated hearings, of veneration. They were, in a word, classical.

Thereafter, living composers competed for place on symphony programs with an ever-growing core of masterpieces by dead ones. To be successful in this increasingly exclusionary system, a living composer had to present works that met four criteria: "lasting value, links to tradition, individuality, and familiarity." In several respects these were contradictory goals, since the more conventional a work was, the less daring, and thus the less likely to achieve distinction in the form of lasting value. And as the orchestra came more and more to represent the traditional values of a perceived conservative upper class, the *avant-garde* composers turned increasingly toward other configurations to premiere their best work.

From their emergence in the 1700s until just after Beethoven, four-movement, abstract symphonies ruled the roost. (And not just by the Austrians and Germans: some sixty volumes of them, composed from 1720 to 1840, from Scandinavia to Rio di Janeiro, were assembled in a collection published in 1986.) Beethoven profoundly changed the rules, not merely with dancing peasants and musical analogues of birds and brooks, but by consistently demanding from his listeners intellectual responses that connected with the extramusical concerns of politics and literature. The Ninth Symphony, with its text of universal brotherhood articulated by a chorus of human voices, was seen as a *summa* of orchestral art—turbulent, terrifying, and, for the next generation of composers trying to get past it, threatening.

In their uneasy coexistence with the testaments of their past, the Romantics and post-Romantics plumbed the possibilities of size and sentiment to be found in the philharmonic orchestra until traditional forms and harmonic functions collapsed under their own weight. Even with traditionalists—say, Brahms, Dvořák, Tchaikovsky—the symphonic processes weakened in their urgency even as they exploded in glamor and size. The breaking free was in full swing by the beginning of World War I, to be measured in the orchestral product coming from beyond Vienna and Bayreuth and Berlin. From the North, for instance, with music of Sibelius and Nielsen; from England and France, with Elgar and Franck and Debussy; even some rumblings from the Americas.

Nobody knew quite what to make of the sometimes harsh sounds to be heard in the symphony hall as the twentieth century advanced, and it is certainly true that audiences took comfort in the accessible modes of such composers as Ravel and Rachmaninov. But it is equally true that Stravinsky had a good following, and that Alban Berg's Violin Concerto of 1935 was understood in many quarters as obviously beautiful. The dumbing-down of the repertoire came from elsewhere. In the metropolitan concert hall, seasoned listeners sat obediently through a new work on nearly every concert—for instance Messiaen's monster *Turangalîla-Symphonie* as premiered by Leonard Bernstein and the Boston Symphony Orchestra in 1949. Sometimes they enjoyed it.

Commissions

Orchestras, soloists, and patrons have long seeded the repertoire by ordering up works for guaranteed performance in a process called commissioning, as in the case of the dark stranger who supposedly commissioned a Requiem Mass from the dying Mozart. The American violinist Louis Krasner commissioned concertos from both Arnold Schoenberg and his disciple Alban Berg; at the height of the British empire, the music publisher Boosey & Hawkes commissioned a set of six *Pomp and Circumstance* marches from Edward Elgar, based on its enthusiasm for the first two—a task that lay unfinished at the composer's death. Given the extraordinary commitment of time to compose and notate works for full orchestra, it is not just the money but the certainty of the performance that makes the system so attractive.

Orchestras embark on ambitious commissioning schemes to celebrate their jubilee anniversaries. Here again the lead was taken in Boston by Serge Koussevitzky, who devoted his wife's considerable fortune from the tea trade to commissioning, performing, and publishing new music. For the orchestra's fiftieth anniversary in 1931, he commissioned the Ravel G-Major Piano Concerto, Roussel's Third Symphony, and Stravinsky's *Symphony of Psalms*. The Koussevitzky Foundation commissioned Bartók's Concerto for Orchestra, for $1,000, as a gesture of support after the composer emigrated to the United States in 1943. For the seventy-fifth anniversary season in 1955–56, the Boston Symphony, Charles Munch, and the Koussevitzky Foundation commissioned some fifteen works, mostly symphonies, from leading American and European composers. Among these were Bernstein's Symphony No. 3 ("Kaddish"), Dutilleux's great Symphony No. 2 ("Le Double"), and Roger Sessions's Symphony No. 3—all still in the repertoire. The Koussevitzky Foundation continues to make important commissions.

Multiple sponsorship is the modern norm. John Adams's 2009 *City Noir* was jointly commissioned by the Los Angeles

Philharmonic, the London Symphony Orchestra, and the Toronto Symphony Orchestra, and was premiered during Dudamel's first concert in Los Angeles. In 2001 a consortium of fifty-eight smaller orchestras in the fifty states was formed to offer those groups enhanced access to newly composed music and first performances, garnering sponsorship from the Ford Motor Company. The composers chosen for the first two rounds of Ford Made in America, Joan Tower and Joseph Schwanter, were safe bets: Tower, known for her *Fanfare for the Uncommon Woman*, and Schwanter, for his Pulitzer Prize (*Aftertones of Infinity* for orchestra, 1979). Tower answered her commission with *Made in America* (2004), a fifteen-minute work, and the subsequent recording by Leonard Slatkin and the Nashville Symphony won three Grammy Awards. The opening credits for the video feature on Schwanter's *Chasing Light* (2007) show the kinds of partnerships that now power the field: the Ford Motor Company Fund, League of American Orchestras, Meet the Composer, National Endowment for the Arts, Aaron Copland Fund for Music, Francis Goelet Charitable Trust, and the Amphion Foundation.

One of the funding angels for another relatively successful multiple-commissioning scheme for regional orchestras boasted that she was out to find "the next Schubert," thereby missing the point.

Historically informed performance

The early music movement began as "ancient music" enthusiasts (primarily in England) dabbled with rebecs and recorders, and it flourished as specialist singers and players found their way, equipped with meticulous reproductions of harpsichords, stringed instruments, and the simpler precursors of modern wind and brass. By the 1960s the movement had reached the early symphonic repertoire, with revelatory concerts and recordings of Vivaldi, Bach, and Handel and steady progress toward the music of the Enlightenment.

The Bach and Handel repertoire had never really died. The annual Three Choirs Festival in southern England claimed a history back to 1719, while Bach was still alive; and a Handel and Haydn Society was founded in Boston in 1815, six years after Haydn's death. But their music lived on in ponderous Romantic versions, as in the popular suite from Handel's *Water Music* arranged by Sir Hamilton Harty, or *The Faithful Shepherd Suite*, freely rendered by Sir Thomas Beecham after Handel's three-act opera, *Il pastor fido:* big-orchestra settings, with clarinets and deadly slow Andantes.

The Concentus Musicus Wien, organized by Nikolaus and Alice Harnoncourt in the mid-1950s, had by 1964 released a pivotal old-instruments performance of the complete Brandenburg Concertos. Neville Marriner's Academy of St. Martin-in-the-Fields made its debut in 1959, typically playing without conductor (but with ordinary modern instruments). Outside Paris, Jean-Claude Malgoire, principal oboist in the new Orchestre de Paris, launched La Grande Écurie et la Chambre du Roy, referencing the horse-mounted wind players and chamber musicians of life at Versailles. The result brought listeners undeniably closer to what these works had sounded like and how they functioned in their own day: Handel's *Royal Fireworks* music, for instance, with a hundred musicians, long on oboes, trumpets, horns, and drums.

And it established a remarkable new market, especially in Britain, where orchestras assembled around the harpsichordists Trevor Pinnock, Christopher Hogwood, and Raymond Leppard. Period-instrument performance moved successfully past Beethoven, led by a clutch of Mozartian fortepianists, Roger Norrington's London Classical Players (1978), and the Hanover Band (1980), so called to evoke Hanoverian period in England, 1714–1830. John Eliot Gardiner launched his Orchestre Révolutionnaire et Romantique in 1990 and was soon working through Berlioz, Schumann, and Mendelssohn on the way forward to Brahms and Verdi.

The music was seizing and controversial. Norrington's performances of Beethoven's Ninth insisted on the composer's surprising and possibly erroneous tempo markings, measurably faster for the slow movement, and much slower for the Turkish March in the finale. There were subtler but not less significant musical results to be heard from the historic seating layouts, faster bow speeds, shorter phrases. Norrington went on to campaign against continuous string vibrato, which he held to be the invention of Fritz Kreisler in the 1930s, robbing the Romantic repertoire, even Mahler, of its "innocence." He was all for applause between movements.

The result is that we now pay little attention to the kind of *Messiah* offered by the Mormon Tabernacle Choir, Philadelphia Orchestra, and Eugene Ormandy in a beloved recording of 1959 (or the slow, slow "Hallelujah" Chorus that concludes a 1963 best-selling *The Joy of Christmas*, with Bernstein, the Philharmonic, and the Mormon Tabernacle Choir), even if we re-hear them with a sense of loving nostalgia. Much as Baroque music became lighter, smaller, livelier, more nuanced, and a great deal more ornamented, Beethoven slow movements taken at their traditional speeds came to be uncomfortably ponderous. Lessons of the "performance practice" movement were assimilated into the world's symphony halls.

But was the result "authentic"? In *Text and Act* (1995) Richard Taruskin, among the most perceptive thinkers of the era, argued that the question was mis-stated: what was at issue had little to do with reviving the past and everything to do with progressive attitudes to performance, which had begun to free live music from the tyrannies of canon.

In 1856 the empress of France, noting only one living composer— Rossini—on a program of the Paris Conservatory Orchestra, asked its nondescript conductor "and does your lovely orchestra play only the work of dead people?" "Madame," he replied with a bow, "the Société des Concerts is the Louvre of Music." He meant it as a compliment: to be canonized is not necessarily to be fossilized. Lawrence Kramer remarks, in *Why Classical Music Still Matters* (2007), "classical music should only be so lucky as to have a museum culture. Museums have become more popular than ever."

At the Brooklyn Academy of Music with its resident Brooklyn Philharmonic Orchestra, Joseph Horowitz substituted, for the subscription series template, weekend festivals built around a theme—"From the New World," "The Russian Stravinsky," "American Transcendalists" (all 1994)—where the anchor concert was surrounded by chamber music, symposiums, and exhibitions. This was much in the style of the new touch-and-learn museology, and it struck a chord. The Brooklyn approach, concluded a writer for *Civilization* magazine, was turning the symphony orchestra from a museum into a community center.

Isms

The Rest Is Noise: Listening to the Twentieth Century, by the *New Yorker* critic Alex Ross, was in music circles easily the book of the year 2007. It laid to rest the notion that "modern music," as last century's repertoire is often dismissed, is anything other than abundant with fascinations. "There is little hope of giving a tidy account" of it, he acknowledges, then invites reader into the myriad offerings of "minimalism, post-minimalism, electronic music, laptop music, Internet Music, New Complexity, Spectralism," and on and on. It is the music, after all, of a half-dozen generations and a hundred cultures: Elliott Carter, for instance, and György Ligeti, Toru Takemitsu, and Magnus Lindberg.

Music-speak had been refreshingly free of the isms that code literary theory and weigh down the squibs seen beside the paintings in an art exhibit (Fauvism, Social Realism, Vortism). There were really only the two big ones, Classicism and Romanticism, until Impressionism and serialism appeared in the vocabulary. Two of the newer isms require attention here, however, because both are directly involved with traditional concerns of orchestral music.

Minimalism describes easily recognized techniques that organize the music of Steve Reich and John Adams. It deals in obsessive repetition of elements, particularly rhythms, that transform as they go, as a bud gains full flower, petal by petal. The orchestral classics are *Short Ride in a Fast Machine* (1986, for the Pittsburgh Symphony) and *The Chairman Dances: Foxtrot for Orchestra* (1985, for the Milwaukee Symphony), an outtake from the opera *Nixon in China*. *Spectralism* describes the compositional approach taken by Gérard Grisey and Tristan Murail at IRCAM, the electronic music component of the Centre Georges Pompidou in Paris. A particular sound cluster, a "chord," is put through computer spectrum analysis, and the components so identified are composed into dense scores of gently shifting colors: consider Grisey's *Les Espaces Acoustiques* (1974–85) and the English composer Brian Ferneyhough's *Plötzlichkeit* for large orchestra (2006). The connection between the two approaches is that both rely on transformations—minimalism, on those of rhythm and meter; spectralism, on those of timbre— descended, in a way, from how themes transform in earlier systems. By turns groovy and then hypnotic, they are "acceptable" and "lasting" because they seem rooted in the natural order of things.

The jury is still out on the multiple marriages of classical and popular styles, "highbrow" and "lowbrow," once called fusion and now widely called crossover. Early examples of the phenomenon are Gershwin's *Rhapsody in Blue*, Ravel's Piano Concerto in G Major, and Milhaud's *La Création du monde*, where jazz, a creeping evil as perceived by the upper classes, instead crept its way into propriety. Techno has joined the minuet at symphony hall. Crossover causes discomfort on both sides of the footlights, but everybody makes discoveries: Mason Bates found orchestral music via Pink Floyd and Radiohead and Bjork albums; London Symphony Orchestra audiences at the 2010–11 performances of Bates's *Mothership* found electronica in full flower.

Today's repertoire is defined not just by the composers-in-residence at the major orchestras (Adams in Los Angeles, Bates in Chicago, Lindberg in New York, Marc-André Dalbavie in Paris and Cleveland) but also by tracks served up from anywhere. Classical composers and performers no longer hide the rock and pop styles they enjoy, while rock musicians can't get enough of *The Rite of Spring.* "What's on your iPod?" Gustavo Dudamel was asked in a press conference, and he talked for five minutes about Latin rhythms and hip goings-on in Spain.

Chapter 7
Commentary

Music journalism was carried in newspapers and magazines from their beginnings, and like conducting, its early practitioners were also composers. Metropolitan orchestra concerts, being noteworthy, got advance listing and subsequent review, sometimes from a dozen or more professional writers. The critics, as though arbiters of public taste, spiritedly argued positions, which usually followed their employer's political and social circumstance. Berlioz earned the bulk of his livelihood writing twice a week for the leading daily paper, the *Journal des Débats*. His particular beat was orchestral music, and over the course of a thirty-year career he had coaxed out of his daily writings a book-length study of the Beethoven symphonies, a text on orchestration and conducting, and a volume of memoirs rich with observations on concert practice of his time. If his Beethoven essays missed the point of sonata form, they nevertheless captured the Romanticism. His treatment of the "Eroica" funeral march praises the dissolution especially: "the shreds of the lugubrious melody, alone, naked, broken, crushed," with the winds "shouting a cry, a last farewell of the warriors to their comrade at arms."

The first major review Robert Schumann wrote for his new paper, the *Neue Zeitschrift für Musik*, 1835, welcomed Berlioz's *Symphonie fantastique*. It is an important piece, attempting to diagram the form of the first movement and refusing the negative position taken by the senior French critic, Fétis. ("He lacks melodic and harmonic ideas.") It makes the connection between Berlioz's narrative approach and Beethoven's. "I confess," Schumann wrote, "that the program at first spoiled my enjoyment, my freedom; but as this faded into the background and my own imagination began to work, I found more than was set down, and almost everywhere in the music a vital glowing tone." His late-career essay, "New Paths," offered his answer to the dilemma of where to find Beethoven's succession: "There must inevitably appear a musician called to give expression to his times in ideal fashion; a musician who would reveal his mastery not in gradual evolution, but like Athene would spring fully armed from Zeus's ear. And such a one has appeared; a young man over whose cradle Graces and Heroes have stood watch. His name is *Johannes Brahms.*"

Music magazines flourished. In Paris a *Revue et Gazette musicale* came from the Schlesinger music publishing empire. In London the *Musical Times*, a monthly, began in 1844 and continues to be a vital presence. In Boston *Dwight's Journal of Music*, published 1851–81, kept its readers abreast of developments abroad as well as activities of the New York Philharmonic, Theodore Thomas's orchestras, and both Boston orchestral societies. Music criticism penned by professional listeners was an integral part of the news cycle. Not infrequently they captured the wind of change in a memorable *aperçu:* "Ho-yo-to-ho," wrote Debussy during the Wagner craze in France; "Lord, how intolerable these people in helmets and animal skins become by the fourth night."

Simply by being there night after night the best critics acquire the vocabulary and experience, and intimate knowledge of the cast of characters, to guide readers into the fundamental debates afoot in orchestral life: the world of reception history, where we read the rise and fall of ideologies and the changing public taste. A few critics gain enormous power and influence. The Viennese critic Eduard Hanslick (1825–1904) spent a lifetime maneuvering readers into accepting a canon of Germanic masterpieces that extended in an

unbroken line from Mozart and Haydn on most directly through
Brahms, master of the absolute in music, a necessary corrective to
the flawed and frivolous world of the stage. Of Wagner's *Tristan und
Isolde*, he held that "the essential factor appears to be the orchestra."

For a hundred years London and New York have enjoyed a
steady diet of the best orchestral fare in the world, on the order
of something important every night. They were the international
capitals of the recording business and remain leaders in
broadcasting. Along with multiple daily papers and some of the
best literary periodicals in any language, there is an educated and
affluent readership. The substance of English-language critical
response devolves from these two places.

At the *New York Herald Tribune*, for instance, the composer-critic
Virgil Thomson led the attack on orchestras as museums: "The
civically supported symphony orchestra is the most conservative
institution in the world. Churches, even banks, are more open to
experiment. The universities are daring by comparison. . . . No
orchestra can live that plays only the music of dead composers."
The *New York Times* had the staff, headed by Olin Downes through
1955 and Harold C. Schonberg through 1980, to cover nearly
everything; elsewhere in the city there were Charles Rosen and
Robert Craft at the *New York Review of Books*, Alan Rich at *New
York* magazine, and a string of first rate-writers at the *New Yorker*
that included London imports Andrew Porter and Desmond Shaw-
Taylor. The New York Music Critics Circle annually announced the
best symphonic composition of the year.

The London tradition of fine writing on music, where criticism and
scholarship routinely find an easy coexistence, descends largely from
Ernest Newman (1868–1959), senior critic of the *Sunday Times*
and author of two dozen books including the four-volume *Wagner
as Man and Artist*. Among his successors at the *Sunday Times*, and
much like Newman in style and approach, was David Cairns, whose
responses, often composed in longhand, got straight to the point:

Karajan, master of half Europe, has conquered London. At the Berlin Philharmonic concerts last week he drove his glittering war chariot over the outstretched necks of the multitude and they loved it. After the Brahms C minor Symphony at the second concert such a deep-throated roar went up as can rarely have been heard in a concert hall. You felt that anyone daring to dissent would be thrown to the horns.

On Mahler's Fourth Symphony

"The drooling and emasculated simplicity of Gustav Mahler! It is not fair to the readers of the *Musical Courier* to take up their time with a detailed description of that musical monstrosity, which masquerades under the title of Gustav Mahler's Fourth Symphony. There is nothing in the design, content, or execution of the work to impress the musician, except its grotesquerie. . . . The writer of the present review frankly admits that . . . to him it was one hour or more of the most painful musical torture to which he has been compelled to submit."—New York *Musical Courier*, November 9, 1904.

Not with a bang but a whisper

"The quiet blessing that ends Mahler's Fourth Symphony receded into silence, and the [Los Angeles] Philharmonic's season was over. . . . The Mahler Fourth was the inspired finale; I can't think of another work that could sound so right after [Ravel's] *L'Enfant et les sortilèges*. [Simon] Rattle moves toward coronation as the new century's first great conductor of Mahler. Like Salonen, he sees the Fourth whole and pure; they both observe the extreme tempo flexibilities throughout—metronome changes sometimes every eight bars—and understand how Mahler meant these changes as a way to create a uniquely lithe and supple melodic line. Rattle has, I think, a surer vision of the work's folksiness: the slides in the strings delicious but ever so slightly obscene, the winds in the scherzo delightfully ill-mannered. Heidi Grant Murphy . . . was the angelic visionary in the fourth movement. The orchestral sound throughout the evening was, well, 'sublime' will do for starters."— Alan Rich, in *So I've Heard*, June 7, 2000.

Music appreciation and musicology

Writers by nature seek to reach the public at large. *How to Listen to Music: Hints and Suggestions to the Untaught Lovers of the Art*, by the New York critic Henry Krehbiel, 1896, sparked an industry. Popularizers like George Marek, a Hungarian emigrant who had risen to become the classical music producer for RCA, wrote *Guiding Your Child to Music, How to Listen to Music Over the Radio*, the *Good Housekeeping Guide to Musical Enjoyment* for readers of the leading ladies' magazine, and several composer biographies with the word "genius" in the title (*Gentle Genius: The Story of Felix Mendelssohn*, 1972). The connection between music appreciation and the sale of RCA records was strong: Charles O'Connell's *Victor Book of the Symphony* (1935), written in the style of his jacket notes, concludes with a list of essential recordings from the single company. The *Music Appreciation Hour*, hosted by the avuncular conductor Walter Damrosch between 1928 and 1942, was broadcast by NBC during school hours and accompanied by teacher guides and pupil workbooks shipped to the schools in advance.

Virgil Thomson dismissed what he called the music-appreciation racket as "a fake-ecstatic, holier-than-thou thing," dangerous because "it is uncritical, in its acceptance of imposed repertory as a criterion of musical excellence." Then the music philosopher Theodor Adorno, serving in a Princeton think tank called the Radio Project (funded by the Rockefeller Foundation and hence connected to NBC), attacked Damrosch and *The Music Appreciation Hour* in a long rant with three dozen footnotes, impugning a system that "exercises a devastating influence by using its own putative unselfishness and altruism as an advertising medium for selfish purposes and vested interests." Middle-class households in the country at large were oblivious to these rumblings. Instead they tuned in ("Good morning, my dear children," Damrosch would begin), purchased record players and records, whistled themes from the great masterworks, and swelled the ranks of the concert-going public.

At colleges and universities, more advanced styles of music appreciation were delivered to the general student populace by engaging, zealous lecturers. The nascent profession of musicology, or music-historical scholarship, flourished after World War II. In their research and writing, late-twentieth-century musicologists refashioned the landscape in terms of factual accuracy and correct scholarly texts of the orchestral repertoire. And they routinely posed critical questions about symphonic music and its meaning: Taruskin, in "Resisting the Ninth," holds that it "is among connoisseurs preeminently the Piece You Love to Hate, no less now than a century and a half ago. Why? Because it is at once incomprehensible and irresistible, and because it is at once awesome and naive." The feminist Susan McClary unleashed a critical firestorm when she suggested that symphonic sonata form and tonality itself were sexist and phallic, and she described the moment of recapitulation of the first movement of the Ninth as exploding "in the throttling murderous rage of a rapist incapable of attaining release."

Program notes

Program notes and liner notes, when knowledgeably prepared, are an essential part of the orchestra experience. The kind of composer commentary placed in programs by Berlioz and Liszt led naturally to third-party explanations, as for instance in early introductions to the Bach passions and the B-Minor Mass. The British composer and theorist Donald Francis Tovey founded the Reid Orchestra in Edinburgh, where he was a professor, and his collected program notes for his group are the basis of his seven-volume *Essays in Musical Analysis* (1935–44). These retain their interest, even a sort of centrality, owing to the author's notion that any concertgoer was capable of hearing and understanding the musical arguments to be presented in the concert hall.

The gentle and genial orchestra commentator Michael Steinberg knew this well, exhorting: "Musical heaven, in any event, is attainable. It offers three sorts of pleasure or delight or nourishment—sensuous, intellectual, and emotional. The perception of sensuous pleasure in music requires no preparation, only clean ears. With experience your receptiveness will become broader, and with it your idea of pleasure. I think of Schoenberg, saying about a passage of delicious idiosyncratic scoring in his Variations for Orchestra, 'I hope that someday these sounds will be found beautiful.'"

Consumed by orchestras and orchestra music, Steinberg led a career that took him from the pages of a major metropolitan newspaper to the pages of the program book in what seems in retrospect a logical path. At the time it was very dramatic indeed: his first review for the *Boston Globe* questioned three of the four divinities of Boston life at the time—the Boston Symphony, Leonard Bernstein, and Charles Munch (but not the Red Sox)— in reviewing the premiere of Bernstein's "Kaddish" Symphony. ("There is something enviable about the utter lack of inhibition with which Leonard Bernstein carries on. His Symphony No. 3 (Kaddish) is a piece, in part, of such unashamed vulgarity, and it is so strongly derivative, that the hearing of it becomes as much as anything a strain on one's credulity.") It seemed he was joining the enemy when he went to work for the BSO in 1976, perfecting a kind of program note the orchestra had long published, and, more significantly, steering the young Seiji Ozawa through the repertoire. Steinberg's career took him thence to San Francisco and Minneapolis, where his wife, the violinist Jorja Fleezanis, was concertmaster. From Minneapolis he continued to write, for Boston, San Francisco, and New York. Oxford University Press in New York published his best program notes in *The Symphony* (1995), *The Concerto* (1998), and *Choral Masterworks* (2005), a collective accomplishment on the order of Tovey's.

Program notes and other forms of audience education could also be delivered live from the podium. The Young People's Concerts of the New York Philharmonic extend back to 1924, and "family concerts" even before that. But it was Leonard Bernstein's flair for them, in the fifty-three televised concerts broadcast from the moment of his arrival in 1958 until 1972, that established the new style of audience education. Bernstein had come to the Philharmonic already a TV personality, having appeared since 1954 in the *Omnibus* series on CBS, with Alistair Cooke as host and the vestiges of the NBC Symphony, now called the Symphony of the Air, as his musicians. The first was a program on sonata form in Beethoven's Fifth, where Bernstein dealt with compositional process as shown in the composer's sketches and stood with his musicians on a giant facsimile of the published score. Some of the Young People's Concerts were composer-centered, as in "Berlioz Takes a Trip," and introductions to Hindemith, Ives, and Copland. Some focused on repertoire niches: jazz, folk music, Latin America. Some were compelling overviews, as in "What Makes Music Symphonic?" and "How to Conduct," the latter with a superb treatment of string bowing and pizzicato.

7. Leonard Bernstein and the New York Philharmonic filming for television in the Great Hall of the Tchaikovsky Conservatory, Moscow, September 1959. The program, including the first movement of Shostakovich's Seventh Symphony, was subsequently broadcast in the United States.

Nearly all of this he planned and wrote himself, as his notes and typescripts show. The rehearsals were early Saturday morning followed by the live broadcast at noon. Children and their parents wrote in from all over the country with adoring thanks. A whole generation of American orchestral musicians made their career choice because of Bernstein and the Young People's Concerts. On the roster of new talent Bernstein himself launched via television may be found the names Michael Tilson Thomas, Yo-Yo Ma, the flutist Paula Robison, the bassist Gary Karr, and the composer Shulamit Ran.

Conductors since have loved the microphone, for better and (often) for worse. David Zinman enjoyed clowning from the stage, on one occasion inviting his trombone players to confess what they think about during the three movements preceding their entry in the Brahms First Symphony. Michael Tilson Thomas's video discs and podcasts in the series *Keeping Score* are much in the Bernstein vein: super program notes for the age of multimedia, with lavish still and moving images and extraordinary readings by the San Francisco Symphony.

After print

Only in London, where a dozen or more fine writers on music still practice and compete for attention, does the newspaper review still flourish. After disappearing from magazines in the 1980s and '90s, music criticism at the dailies collapsed with the rest of the industry beginning in about 2005. Chicago's senior critic Wynne Delacoma was edged out of her job with the *Chicago Sun-Times*, replaced by "a handful of freelancers"; in 2007 the *Atlanta Journal-Constitution* seemed to release its classical music critic, Pierre Ruhe, in a reorganization affecting forty staff members; *New York* magazine forced out Peter G. Davis, 71, after twenty-five years' worth of solid work. Since all three cities were homes to major symphony and opera companies, the outcry was fierce. Robert Spano, the music director of the Atlanta Symphony

Orchestra, wrote the *Journal-Constitution* that their action would "distinguish Atlanta as the largest city in the country without a classical music, book or art critic on staff at its major newspaper. . . . Art matters." The papers responded with a good deal of back-pedaling, Atlanta rather lamely insisting that "Ruhe's status was never really in jeopardy." A spokesperson at *New York* magazine countered, circuitously, "It's an important category for us to continue robust criticism in." But the stampede was on and did not let up. Melinda Bargreen, critic of three decades' duration for the *Seattle Times*, was bought out in 2008; in Los Angeles Alan Rich (1924–2010), who over fifteen years wrote some of the best criticism going on anywhere, was simply fired from *LA Weekly*. "It's open season on critics," he wrote. "We are an endangered species."

It was understatement for the *New York Times* to suggest that all this had "flustered the profession, which views robust analysis, commentary and reportage as vital to the health of the art form. But the changes have also disturbed the people who run musical institutions like opera houses and orchestras, several of whom have protested to local editors."

For some the promise of the World Wide Web predated the collapse of the newspaper industry, with the result that Internet-based venues for music criticism were already alive and well as the newspapers bowed out. Robert Commanday, critic for the *San Francisco Chronicle* (1965–93) and dean of Bay Area critics, chose as his retirement project to establish an e-zine called *San Francisco Classical Voice*, jointly with the philanthropist Gordon Getty, in 1998. The writers were invited professional musicians with something to say, compensated by their concert tickets and a modest fee. *SFCV*, constrained neither by word count nor geographic boundary, became the journal of record for classical music in northern California, its Tuesday-morning appearances online widely anticipated. It its first year, Commanday himself wrote the best reports on the sleazy symphonic goings-on in Sacramento, the state capital, under the headline "Trouble in River City."

American newspapers, and to a lesser extent the British as well, eventually gave up the pretense of wanting a role in the literature of classical music: in most American cities the one-hundredth birthday in 2008 of orchestral composer Elliott Carter passed unremarked—though in Washington, at least, he was given a Presidential Medal of Freedom. The void was filled, zealously, on the Internet, which had been the most interesting forum for record reviews since *High Fidelity / Stereo Review* petered out in the mid '90s. With audio and video clips and no holds barred, the blogs of 2005 and beyond first overcame the limitations of the newspaper, and then served as the model for a new kind of arts commentary. Alan Rich launched a blog before his death, *So I've Heard* (2008), where the masthead reads, defiantly, "Writing about music, like the art itself, is alive and well in this country." And optimistic, as he describes the arrival of Gustavo Dudamel with the LA Philharmonic and its new home:

> We have a marvelous orchestra on our hands, a phenomenal talent on its podium, an audience that, so far at least, simply radiates satisfaction and good will, a quality unique these days in the large concert halls of the world. It is a lovely gesture, and a not insignificant one, that Gustavo prefers to take his bows in close communion with the orchestra members. "We're in this together," he seems to say, and there is no better way to shape a great symphony orchestra.

Alex Ross has *The Rest Is Noise*; Joseph Horowitz, *The Unanswered Question*. Norman Lebrecht, who fought blogs all the way, now writes a good one, *Slipped Disc*. In Atlanta, the "unsinkable" Pierre Ruhe, to use Ross's formulation, unveiled *Arts Critic ATL*.

Chapter 8
Recordings

Mechanical reproduction of sound has been around a long time, since the concept extends to the music boxes and barrel organs for which Haydn and Mozart composed new music. Simply by establishing the supposed speed of a movement, the metronome (an invention of the 1810s) took listeners sharply closer to the composer's true world. In 1889, visiting Gustave Eiffel's private study at the top of the Eiffel Tower, Thomas Edison demonstrated the latest version of his decade-old talking machine. Although the two visionaries listened that day to live music (Charles Gounod at the piano), Edison, thinking his invention useful for secretaries and elocution lessons, failed to envisage the music industry just around the corner.

In 1898 the American recording engineer Fred Gaisberg arrived in England to oversee flat-disc recordings for the new Gramophone Company. "His Master's Voice" as heard by Nipper the dog was a familiar trademark by 1900. Arthur Nikisch's discs of Beethoven's Fifth with the Berlin Philharmonic, arguably the first successful recordings of a major orchestra, are from 1913. Experiments with recording members of the Chicago and Cincinnati orchestras were not long coming, and in October 1917, both the Boston Symphony with Karl Muck and the Philadelphia Orchestra with Leopold Stokowski had traveled to the Victor Corporation's headquarters in Camden, New Jersey, to essay the first recordings for full orchestra.

Boston recorded ten sides, including the Hungarian March from Berlioz's *Damnation de Faust* and Wolf-Ferrari's *Secret of Suzanne* overture. The Philadelphia, taking the ferry across the river two weeks later, recorded two Brahms Hungarian Dances. Muck's Berlioz, a portion of which can be heard spliced together with later recordings by Koussevitzky and Munch in a 1956 seventy-fifth-anniversary release, is solid, conservative, strict-tempoed even to the end; Stokowski's Brahms, fluid and fascinating in the suddenness of its speed changes. By the end of World War I a serious repertoire was commercially available for purchase. In 1918 the Paris Conservatory Orchestra waited out the flu epidemic in New York by cutting discs for Columbia, some fifteen in all including their signature repertoire of works by Bizet, Saint-Saëns, Delibes, and André Messager.

But it was the invention and spectacularly rapid deployment of the electric microphone and loudspeakers in the 1920s—again a direct marker of postwar prosperity—that so altered the profile and bankbook of orchestras from the 1920s through the 1990s: a golden era, lasting some seventy-five years. Records were the postwar outcome, in one sense, of *fin-de-siècle*'s glittering symphonic life. Take, for instance, Stokowski, the Philadelphia Orchestra, and its concertmaster Thaddeus Rich in Saint-Saëns's *Danse macabre* in 1925, with its clarity of sound and correct instrumentation, the first electrical recording of a symphony orchestra. "Here, finally, was real music," wrote one of the architects, "miraculous in fidelity and warmth—and we were only at the beginning." Or the syrupy portamentos of Ravel's 1920 *La Valse*, recorded in 1927 by Philippe Gaubert and the Paris Conservatory Orchestra (French Columbia) just after the new equipment arrived abroad. Ravel himself conducted *Boléro* with the Lamoureux Orchestra for Polydor in 1930, not long after its composition.

By 1930 there had developed a headlong international competition to record and package the orchestral masterworks. The big record labels—RCA Red Seal, Columbia, EMI (Electric and Musical

Industries, Ltd.), later DGG and Philips—vied with enormous capital expenditures for exclusive contracts with orchestras and their conductors. This was repeated again in the late 1940s and early '50s with the dawn of long-playing disc format, and yet again with stereo, the triumph of the 1960s. All the great orchestras were involved, and not a few conductors—Bruno Walter, Pierre Monteux, Ernest Ansermet, Charles Munch, and Stokowski—were around for all three cycles.

Electricity

The electrification of the great cities brought with it the radio, which within five years of the widespread public broadcasting that began in 1922 had devastated the market for acoustic recording. A million Americans tuned in for the first live broadcast of a symphony orchestra, the BSO under Koussevitzky, October 9, 1926, on the NBC affiliate station WBZ. The first of the powerful German radio orchestras, in Leipzig, began to broadcast in 1934, followed by the Berlin Radio Orchestra just later. The BBC Symphony was established in 1930. Microphones were hung in the world's concert halls. Orchestra players, one by one, took time off to hear what they sounded like on the radio.

Either one of these developments—broadcasting and electric recording—would have revolutionized the philharmonic. Together they redefined concert music just as surely as opening concerts to the public did in the eighteenth century. The ability of radio to reach into every home staggered the imagination. The record player and radio, designed to complement the latest in interior decoration, drew listeners away from the piano in the parlor to what became the living room. Dreamers began to imagine a time when every citizen would know the instruments of the orchestra and sonata form. Aaron Copland's *Music for Radio* (1937) was composed for a naming contest held by the CBS Symphony and drew more than a thousand entries, from which the composer chose "Saga of the Prairie." Orchestral music on radio and, shortly, television flourished not just with the NBC Symphony but with high-profile sponsorships like *The Voice of Firestone* (1928–53) and the *Bell Telephone Hour* (1940–58). The Philadelphia Orchestra was the first to be broadcast on television, thirty minutes earlier than the New York Philharmonic (March 20, 1948), just after James Petrillo had lifted the union embargo. Classical music broadcasting continues to be healthy on public radio, established by the Public Broadcasting Act of 1967 (NPR for radio, PBS for television, and the Corporation for Public Broadcasting to distribute funding to the local stations) and on the national good-music stations abroad, now streaming on the Web.

The movies romanticized the orchestra in several ways, nowhere more so than Walt Disney's *Fantasia* (1940), which brought a new young public to the orchestra. Mickey Mouse shakes hands with Stokowski after *The Sorcerer's Apprentice*, connecting the old ways to the new with stirring power. So, too, did Disney's animated *Peter and the Wolf* (1946), shown as a short subject before screenings of *Fantasia*. Some of the dozens of orchestra-based movies have fleeting moments of getting it right: consider Jean-Louis Barrault's Berlioz in *La Symphonie Fantastique* (1942), Katharine Hepburn's Clara Schumann in *Song of Love* (1947); some stretches of *Amadeus* (1984), *Immortal Beloved* (1994), and *The Red Violin* (1998).

The recording industry: The Big Three

Even limited to how it involved orchestras, the saga of mergers and buyouts and brilliant, sometimes devious capitalists that describes the record industry defies summary. The three principal players were RCA with its prestige Red Seal label, Columbia Masterworks, and the London-based EMI, formed in 1931 from the merger of the Gramophone (HMV and French Pathé) and Columbia Graphophone companies, and operating from studios in Abbey Road.

Working his magic from London with the new EMI, Fred Gaisberg scored two great coups just before the outbreak of World

War II and emigration: records of Szell, Casals, and the Czech Philharmonic in the Dvořák Cello Concerto (1937) and Bruno Walter conducting Mahler's Ninth live from the Vereinssaal, January 16, 1938, just a few weeks before the Anschluss in March. (Gaisberg took the proof copies to Paris, where Walter had relocated.) He also discovered and cultivated Walter Legge to be his successor at EMI. Legge had the theory that recordings, properly engineered and with liberal retakes, should sound better than live performances and therefore become the benchmarks for classical music. He set out to produce those benchmarks by contracting to his label the best of the world's performers.

Together with Sir Thomas Beecham, and with an eye toward dominating London orchestral music after World War II, Legge founded the Philharmonia Orchestra in 1945, then after a rupture with Beecham, administered it himself. At the war's end he was in Vienna, signing both Karajan and Furtwängler to the Philharmonia and EMI; he subsequently lured into his stable Toscanini, Richard Strauss, Maria Callas, and Elisabeth Schwarzkopf, whom he married. Legge was the agent of Karajan's quick postwar rehabilitation, engaging him to appear with the Philharmonia live and on record from 1948 through 1960. Under Karajan the Philharmonia, thought Legge, reached "a new and higher standard of performance than Britain has ever had."

When Karajan went to Berlin in 1954, Legge coached Otto Klemperer, turning seventy, into a brilliant end-of-career run. And when Legge broke with EMI and tried to dissolve the Philharmonia, Klemperer successfully led it into becoming a musicians' cooperative, the New Philharmonia. This is the group heard in Mahler's *Das Lied von der Erde*, with Christa Ludwig and Fritz Wunderlich, recorded in the early 1960s and re-released in EMI's admired CD series, Great Recordings of the Century. Klemperer was no particular fan of the industry, having famously remarked that "Listening to a recording is like going to bed with a photograph of Marilyn Monroe." Walter Legge's effect on orchestra music continues to be debated. To the London critic Andrew Porter, who was there, Legge raised standards everywhere and permanently.

RCA Victor assumed its modern configuration in 1929, when the Radio Corporation of America absorbed the Victor Talking Machine Co., with its trademark Red Seal label and "His Master's Voice" motto. (RCA continued its affiliation with British Gramophone Company, which used the same trademarks, such that its founder, David Sarnoff, was on the board of the new EMI when it was formed; RCA sold its share of EMI in 1931, but American RCA recordings continued to be distributed abroad by EMI on the HMV label.) RCA's principal orchestras were the Boston Symphony under Koussevitzky and the Philadelphia under Stokowski, with some titles from the Chicago Symphony under Frederick Stock. Stokowski and the Philadelphia, proximate to RCA's sprawling establishment in Camden, had been the backbone of Victor classical offerings since 1917, eventually reaching past waltzes and light classics to two accounts of Schubert's "Unfinished" Symphony (1925) and to symphonies of Franck, Dvořák, and Tchaikovsky. Koussevitzky's three-disc Prokofiev recording in April 1929 was one of the first publications with the new RCA Victor label, followed by an epoch-defining Tchaikovsky Pathétique (Symphony No. 6), recorded April 14–16, 1930, in Symphony Hall, and the very first Mussorgsky *Pictures at an Exhibition*, a Koussevitzky commission to which he retained the performance rights.

The Depression crippled the industry in the United States and abroad, with virtually no significant recording programs between 1930 and 1934. Between the introduction of radio and the interwar recovery, record sales fell from over $105 million to $5.5 million annually. Classical recording powered back up in early 1935, with recording sessions in Boston Symphony Hall for Strauss's *Also sprach Zarathustra*, Mendelssohn's "Italian" Symphony, and Sibelius's Second. "One hour of one recording session will be broadcast," announced an invitation to Boston patrons. "It will thus be possible to hear the orchestra playing while the records are actually being made. The studio procedure will also be explained."

David Sarnoff became president of RCA in 1930 and after extracting a freestanding company (from Westinghouse and General Electric), proceeded to shape the new generation of electronic communication, where records, radio networks, and television were all in the master plan. On Christmas night 1937, the seventy-year-old Arturo Toscanini led the first program of the new NBC Symphony in Rockefeller Center's Studio 8-H, remodeled for the occasion. There and in Carnegie Hall, in weekly broadcasts and a steady stream of records, the NBC juggernaut carried on through Toscanini's retirement in the spring of 1954. The dream roster of NBC Symphony musicians figured prominently in orchestra affairs for decades more: among the half-dozen celebrity violinists Josef Gingold, who later taught Jaime Laredo and Joshua Bell; the violist William Primose and cellist Leonard Rose; three ace bassoonists, Elias Carmen, Leonard Sharrow, and Arthur Weisberg; and on through the ranks. So, too, did the discography, which ran to eighty-two volumes when released on CD as *The Arturo Toscanini Collection* (1990). The Beethoven cycle became the one against which later ones were judged; the pounding opening of the Brahms First Symphony is lodged in the ears of everyone who heard it.

In 1938 William Paley at the Columbia Broadcasting System purchased the historic American Columbia record label for $750,000. The first Columbia Masterworks recording was the Brahms Symphony No. 1 with Felix Weingartner and the (old) Royal Philharmonic Orchestra, followed by new recordings from Minneapolis, under Mitropoulos, and New York, now the New York Philharmonic-Symphony, under Rodzinski, Walter, Szell, and others. Columbia was the first label to settle with Petrillo and the AFM, in November 1944, taking as a trophy the Philadelphia

Orchestra with Eugene Ormandy, and an upper hand in the race for other niches including the spoken word (Edward R. Murrow's *Hear It Now*) and Broadway original-cast albums.

Columbia's signal triumph came when it introduced a viable long-playing format, a 12-inch disc at 33⅓ rpm, in 1948 while RCA was promoting its 45-rpm, "extended play" system, with discs of roughly the same capacity as the old 78s. The 12-inch LP could hold more than twenty minutes on a side and was thus capable of playing symphonic movements uninterrupted by a record change. That this was Columbia's niche repertoire with the Philadelphia and New York orchestras had been grasped early on by the leading promoter of the LP, Godard Lieberson (1911–77). The first classical LP was the Mendelssohn Violin Concerto with Nathan Milstein, Bruno Walter, and the New York Philharmonic-Symphony, Columbia ML-4001. RCA capitulated in 1950, leaving 45s as the medium of choice for pop singles.

LPs and stereo

At Columbia, Lieberson continued to redraw the field of play. As an intellectual and composer, he thought it obvious that the high-profit Broadway recordings (the best-selling *My Fair Lady*, for instance, 1956) should support less viable ventures: the work of living Americans, Shostakovich and Schoenberg and Webern, early electronic music, Glenn Gould. He offered Bernstein, just arriving at the New York Philharmonic, an unrestricted twenty-year contact. If these did not make as much money as Ormandy and the Philadelphia, they were just as long on glamour. Among discophiles the 1967 Bernstein / New York boxed set of Mahler symphonies was the prestige purchase of the year.

RCA's engineers, led by the visionary John Pfeiffer, developed workable techniques for recording in stereo, beginning with an experimental taping in Boston of the "Ride to the Abyss" from Berlioz's *La Damnation de Faust* in 1956. They gained the corporate upper hand by deciding to proceed before it was clear how stereophonic sound would reach the consumer. (The first stereo publications were released as reel-to-reel tape.) With a distinctive Living Stereo trademark and new serial numbers beginning LSC, RCA stereo dominated the market again, for instance the "Stereo Spectacular" with Charles Munch conducting the Boston Symphony in the Saint-Saëns "Organ" Symphony, 1959.

In postwar England, Decca (marketed in the United States as London Records) was quick to embrace the vinyl LP format and first to use high-fidelity equipment enabling "full frequency range response" or *ffrr*. It developed a simple contraption for hanging three omnidirectional microphones, the "Decca tree." The brilliant producer John Culshaw (1924–80) gambled the company on a complete studio recording of Wagner's *Ring* with Georg Solti that turned out to be a financial and artistic hit. Culshaw also produced the great 1963 recording of Benjamin Britten's *War Requiem* with the composer conducting. With Karajan and the Vienna Philharmonic there was a major series including Mozart and Beethoven, Grieg, ballet music, Holst's *The Planets*, and the Strauss tone poems. These were released on CD on the occasion of the conductor's centenary in 2008 as *Karajan: The Legendary Decca Recordings.*

Deutsche Grammophon Gesellschaft, having been acquired before World War II by the Siemens conglomerate, was led into postwar recovery by Elsa Schiller. In 1959 she signed Herbert von Karajan and the Berlin Philharmonic, certainly the most lucrative single contract in recording history. The marriage yielded more than 300 recordings of extreme artistry and, because they were expensive imports in most markets, snob value. The cycle of nine Beethoven symphonies released in 1962, at $40 (roughly $300 in 2010 purchasing power), had no rivals. On Schiller's retirement, Karajan effectively became the artistic administrator of DGG and was personally responsible for 20 percent of the world classical market. Beginning in the 1950s the Dutch Philips corporation actively sought mergers destined to bring it to effective competition with EMI, with the result that DGG and Philips merged in 1962, formally renamed PolyGram a decade later. PolyGram began to distribute London/Decca in the United States in 1980.

Magnetic tape, a product of the military-industrial complex, was universally adopted in the recording industry by the late 1950s. Tape, owing to the simplicity of the medium, brought with it the technique of splicing to perfection, radically altering the process of retakes. Tape was much more easily reproduced than a disc, making possible limited publication of performances that lacked a mass market. The American Recording Project, headed by Aaron Copland, evaluated tapes of orchestral performances of new music and, after recommending a few for commercial publication, saw to the deposit of multiple copies of the tapes in major public libraries.

For orchestras, the stereo LP boom lasted just short of two decades before saturating a dwindling market. RCA dropped new orchestral recordings in 1973. By 1980 the end of the big-label contracts with the major orchestras had been reached. Classical music no longer broke even, and drew only 5 percent of record sales, while popular music from the Beatles and Elvis Presley to hard rock was drawing $9 billion in a year. The new-wave record executives were not fans. Classical recording's two megastars died within months of one another, Karajan in 1989 and Bernstein in 1990.

Digits

The compact disc had two principal advantages: it was sturdier than vinyl—record libraries had to replace their Szell/Cleveland sets every year or so, owing to the scratches—and it held nearly three times the length of a stereo face. People jettisoned collections of old vinyl to buy the same recordings a second or third time, thus briefly breaking the free-fall in the market for new recordings. Short-run labels and (mostly pirated) computer re-engineerings of historic artifacts made a little profit. There were some obvious limitations: at EMI it was properly asked "How will we ever

Recordings

persuade people to buy another Beethoven cycle when the one they have got will last forever?" Attention turned to the potential of the master recordings in the vaults.

Sony, the Japanese colossus, proceeded to walk away with the recording industry. Both Akio Morita, one of the founders, and his successor Norio Ohga were music lovers with a keen sense for the symbiosis of hardware and media. Ohga and Karajan, both licensed jet pilots, were good friends, and Ohga a sometime conductor. The Philips cassette tape and Sony Walkman brought true portability to the consumer market, leading in due course to the Philips/Sony workgroup that developed the CD. The first test CD, with Karajan conducting Richard Strauss's *Alpine Symphony*, was pressed in Hanover in 1981, and a new factory was in operation the following year at PolyGram, the Philips-DGG-Decca consortium, not far from where the first flat discs had been made. In the aftershock of the stock market crash of October 1987, Sony, requiring content for its technology, purchased Columbia Records for $2 billion. RCA was absorbed into the Bertelsmann Music Group (BMG), then BMG became part of the Sony empire in 2004. Ohga's personal reach into orchestral affairs was substantial, particularly at the Boston Symphony, where Seiji Ozawa was conductor. The BSO's supposed reliance on Japanese philanthropy was said to explain Ozawa's having kept his job as long as he did.

Naxos Records, founded in 1987 by Klaus Heymann and based in Hong Kong, again redefined classical music recording. By using orchestras in Bratislava and Ljubljana, Naxos could make a profit on a few thousand sales of $6 discs. In less than a decade Naxos was publishing 300 records a year and had sold 10 million—classical, esoterica, old classics recovered. The economics were good all around since a central European player drawing $100 extra pay for each disc recorded saw real improvements in lifestyle, while Naxos avoided the high costs of fixed union contracts in the majors.

Classical music also enjoyed some hits, like Górecki's Third Symphony with soprano Dawn Upshaw (Nonesuch, 1992), which reached no. 6 on the pop charts and became the first classical recording to sell a million copies; and Nigel Kennedy's recording of Vivaldi's *The Four Seasons* (EMI, 1989), which eventually sold two million. Then came *The Three Tenors*, auctioned to Warner Music Group for £11 million.

The first and to some extent most interesting response of the big orchestras, as their contracts evaporated, was to issue their own labels, available from their gift shops, catalogs, and eventually by Internet. The label *LSO Live* began in 2000 with a new Berlioz cycle from Colin Davis and the London Symphony in time for the composer's bicentennial in 2003. (The first Colin Davis Berlioz Cycle, on Philips, had coincided with the centennial of Berlioz's death, in 1969.) Works are recorded live during every concert in the series, then are edited and mixed in postproduction. In 2010–11 the catalog numbered seventy discs, with impressive projects by Davis, Bernard Haitink, and Valery Gergiev—something approaching the rhythm of the best days of stereo.

SFS Media, the San Francisco Symphony's in-house label, launched its highly praised Mahler cycle in 2001 and finished it in 2010, after sales of nearly 150,000 copies and a clutch of Grammy awards. In Boston, Philadelphia, and Chicago there have been major retrospectives issued on the occasion of the centenaries of their symphony halls, largely from archival tapes of radio broadcasts. A sturdy market has sprung up for DVDs of historical television broadcasts.

Digital music stores and streaming audio and video on orchestra websites achieve the kinds of technological advances every season that records did in the 1950s and '60s. Easily the most compelling solution in 2011 was the Berlin Philharmonic's Digital Concert Hall, documenting every conceivable detail of the concert season in video of breathtaking beauty, captured by six remote-controlled

HD cameras unobtrusively installed at the Philharmonie. Unlimited access to the current broadcasts and the archive sold for €149 for a twelve-month subscription.

No single listener could possibly keep up. Two decades after the Three Tenors, the collapse of the classical record industry seemed more in the nature of a correction. The winner was the public, with a boundless supply of serious listening at its beck and call, and virtually unlimited access to the daily life of orchestras anywhere in the world.

Chapter 9
Peace

Connections between music and politics were obvious enough to the first orchestral musicians, attached as many of them were to princely retinues and military bands. Allusions to the civilization-changing events of revolution and empire pepper Haydn's symphonies (and the "Dona nobis pacem" movements from the "Lord Nelson" Mass and "Mass in Time of War"), and there is surely no greater music for a fallen military hero than the second movement of Beethoven's Third ("Eroica," 1803). The military nuance of the Janissary band and swagger of the hero's strophe in the fourth movement of the Ninth are unmistakable, arguments that complicate the way we hear the subsequent strophe on mankind embraced as brothers beneath the star-canopied gaze of a loving father.

The orchestra's potential as agent of peace among people of good will is obvious too. It embodies concord and community and has as its raison d'être the pursuit of beauty. There is an eerie sensed current of cultural imperialism when it comes to sending orchestras on missions abroad at phenomenal expense. But the motives are generally honorable and the results sometimes lasting. Touring instruments of peace are in any event far less expensive than the cheapest act of war.

Orchestras took naturally to the railroad. Trains accommodated groups of 80 or 100 players and attendant drayage with ease, and by the 1850s were fast connecting the cultural capitals. The first orchestra to travel widely was the Berlin Philharmonic, to France and Switzerland in the spring of 1897, Russia in 1899, and the United States in 1912. The Lamoureux Orchestra from Paris reached London in 1896; the London Symphony Orchestra visited Paris in 1906 and Antwerp in 1908. New York was easily accessible by rail for the Boston, Chicago, and Philadelphia orchestras, which traveled regularly to Carnegie Hall. Festivals and fairs also drew full orchestras away from home. In 1900 Mahler took the Vienna Philharmonic to play Beethoven's "Eroica" and Fifth symphonies in Paris on the occasion of the Exposition Universelle, one of the most successful world's fairs ever, even though they left Austria without the wherewithal to get back.

The city of Strasbourg lies at the heart of Europe and at the confluence of French and German culture. Here, during a three-day orchestral festival in May 1905, Richard Strauss and the Lamoureux's conductor Camille Chevillard shared the first concert, and Mahler and Strauss another: Mahler's Fifth and Strauss's *Sinfonia domestica* (and two other works) on the same monster program. ("Mahler monopolized all the rehearsal time," Strauss grumbled.) Mahler led the closing all-Beethoven concert, with Ferruccio Busoni playing the Fourth Piano Concerto and what was by all accounts an unforgettable Ninth Symphony. "I have never before heard Beethoven's Ninth like that," wrote one critic, "and Strasbourg has never before heard such a storm of applause. . . . Mahler the conductor is the Napoleon of the baton."

In the days before recording and broadcasting, these cultural encounters were reckoned to have immense artistic and diplomatic potential. On one of the few leisure afternoons they could have had in Strasbourg, Strauss played Mahler his still-unfinished score of *Salome*, leaving the latter "utterly convinced" of its merits and stimulating Mahler's long and unsuccessful battle to get the opera past the Viennese censors. Georges Clemenceau, within a few months to be president of France, rescued Mahler from a crush of admirers after the Beethoven concert.

With Germany and France at war, Felix Weingartner and the Darmstadt Orchestra encountered André Messager and the Paris Conservatory Orchestra on the platform of the railway station in Bern, Switzerland. "Since this was neutral territory," a journalist reported, "weapons stayed in their cases." Meanwhile, Alfred Cortot at the new French arts propaganda agency, Action Artistique, contrived to send the Conservatory Orchestra on a tour of the United States to boost Franco-American relations. The chief financial backer was the great American financier and philanthropist Otto Kahn. The tour turned into a victory celebration when the Armistice was proclaimed just as the orchestra reached Washington and Richmond. It continued on through the South and Midwest to California and back, with programs showing the Stars and Stripes crossed with the *tricolore*, and with freshly pressed copies of their new Columbia records on sale in the lobby. This was recognized in the minutes as *propagande à l'américaine*.

World War II

Among cultured Europeans the primacy of German-speaking composers, Hanslick's canonic lineage from Bach through Haydn and Mozart to Beethoven and in some quarters Brahms, was essentially a matter of faith. Beethoven was a marker of cultural superiority just as surely as the French turned to Joan of Arc and the English to Shakespeare. Among Hitler's favorite composers were both Beethoven and Bruckner, but Wagner's message spoke loudest to him, with the result that the bulk of the music-specific propaganda radiated not from the concert hall but from Bayreuth. Beethoven had long been owned by the world at large, and while monster forces assembled in Berlin to play the Ninth for Hitler's birthday in April 1942, filmed before floor-to-ceiling swastika banners and wounded soldiers in uniform, at the same time the motto opening of the Fifth Symphony was the sound bite for Churchill's "V for Victory."

Racial cleansing had already resulted in the dismissal of Paul Hindemith, Bruno Walter, George Szell, Georg Solti, Mahler's protégé Otto Klemperer, and a host of instrumentalists from their posts in Germany and its conquests. The work of Jewish composers was prohibited from public performance: Mendelssohn and Mahler, of course, and in occupied France the list extended to Chopin, the Russians, Ravel, and all unpublished music by living French composers. The Berlin Philharmonic under Furtwängler became the Reichsorchester. The Gewandhaus Orchestra was sent touring as an ambassador of National Socialism, conducted by Hermann Abendroth, who had joined the Nazi party in 1937, and the young Herbert von Karajan.

Metropolitan orchestras in the occupied nations were understood to be necessities of cultural life, on a par with playhouses and the movies. Occupiers saw the continuation of these things as proof that the good life could go on; the occupied, as a way of steering souls through troubled times and garnering at least some income. Conductors and soloists were forced into making critical choices, with little time for sober reflection and only vague guesses as to what the future might bring. Toscanini, who had already been conducting for a half century and been the first non-German to conduct in Bayreuth, turned aggressively anti-Fascist and by 1939 refused to appear in Italy, Germany, Vienna, or Salzburg. The French pianist Cortot, by contrast, preached German superiority and played in Berlin. Furtwängler, caught in the vise, maneuvered through one pragmatic response after another—on the one hand never actually becoming court conductor to Hitler's Berlin, but at the same time unable to hide a streak of anti-Semitism and an ego that itself bordered on the dictatorial.

Collaboration with the Third Reich was measured, after the war as the "purification" rituals took their course, in terms of who had

8. Wilhelm Furtwängler conducts the Berlin Philharmonic in
Beethoven's Ninth Symphony for Hitler's birthday, April 19, 1942.

played in Berlin or on the Nazi-controlled radio and who was photographed with enemy soldiers. There was nothing systematic about the judgments. Toscanini returned to Italy cast as a war hero. Furtwängler took refuge in Switzerland, from which exile he furtively appeared from time to time as the years passed. Karajan successfully weathered the postwar storm since he was central to the business interests of the London recording industry. André Cluytens, who had positively enjoyed his interaction with German forces in Bordeaux, rose to the top of the Paris establishment, and soon had engagements in Bayreuth and Vienna. British and American orchestras were the big winners, of course, not only with Szell and Munch and Solti and a dozen like them but with hundreds of players who had managed to find their way out.

The Cold War

What came to be called cultural diplomacy secured its earliest and perhaps greatest victory when the Boston Symphony Orchestra traveled to the Soviet Union in September 1956. It was the BSO's second trip abroad, part of its seventy-fifth anniversary season, beginning with Ireland and the Edinburgh Festival and proceeding after Leningrad and Moscow on to Vienna and Munich, Paris and London. The Russian itinerary was inserted a few days after President Eisenhower's plea before NATO, the summer before, to lift the Iron Curtain. The Boston players were shuttled from Helsinki to Leningrad in a caravan of small Aeroflot craft, improvising as they went. Concerts were added to meet the demand, and the results greeted with rapture from every quarter. The Soviet composer Dmitri Kabalevsky wrote in *Pravda* of how "we heard the real Beethoven—the great leader of humanitarian ideas—of beauty and freedom who leads us through difficult paths towards his ideals."

The musical elite were all there: Shostakovich, Kabalevsky, Khachaturian, the Oistrakhs, Kiril Kondrashin, the young Rostropovich. Russian players met their Boston counterparts backstage. Vladimir Ashkenazy remembers the Boston visit as the

9. Charles Munch conducts the Boston Symphony Orchestra in Leningrad, September 6, 1956.

high point of his conservatory studies; Kurt Sanderling, Mravinsky's longtime associate conductor, soon left Russia to pursue an international career. A Russian violinist who later went to the San Francisco Symphony was impressed that the Bostonians, players and their conductor alike, arrived at rehearsal wearing open shirts and slacks, tuning and conversing onstage. In the aftermath President Eisenhower saluted the orchestra for demonstrating "one of the most effective methods of strengthening world friendship." And it was true that the Iron Curtain had been rent: the following season, leading Russian orchestral composers arrived in the United States, and the season after that Van Cliburn won the first International Tchaikovsky Music Competition in Moscow.

The money for the BSO tour had come more or less directly from the CIA, through a wholesomely named American Committee for Cultural Freedom. "We couldn't spend it all," said a former agent.

The Iron Curtain was no longer an obstacle either for Western touring orchestras or for those from the Soviet Union. The Leningrad Philharmonic played in western Europe in 1956, London in 1960, and the United States in 1962. The BSO was aloft again in 1960, on a six-week Pacific tour that centered on thirteen concerts in Japan, a nation hooked on radio and television—and soon mass-producing Yamaha pianos and orchestral instruments—and eager to acquire all the Western music it could. The players wept at the new Peace Museum in Hiroshima and witnessed first-hand the devastation of the tsunami that reached Japan after the great earthquake in Chile on May 22, 1960. (In 2011, the Manchester-based BBC Philharmonic was touring Japan when the March earthquake and tsunami struck as their buses crossed a suspension bridge to Yokohama; the last four of their ten concerts were canceled, and the orchestra straggled home.)

The Philadelphia Orchestra, trumped in its desire to be the first to reach the USSR because of union issues at home, sought to turn the tables at the next opportunity. Shortly after "ping-pong diplomacy" in China had made the headlines in 1971, Eugene Ormandy wrote to President Nixon proposing the availability of his orchestra to travel there, a proposal that figured in the secret visit of Henry Kissinger to China in July 1971 and in the presidential visit in 1972. Ormandy was for different reasons acceptable both to the Chinese and to Richard Nixon, himself a classical music connoisseur and sometime pianist. In the end it was agreed to allow a single Boeing-707 aircraft, seating 140, into the People's Republic of China—104 players and crew, and a dozen officials and members of the press. The orchestra presented six concerts in Beijing and Shanghai in September 1973, its programs having been selected by a committee: the national anthems, Beethoven, Roy Harris's Third Symphony, the *Yellow River Concerto*, and *Stars and Stripes Forever*. At the concert in the Great Hall of the People in Beijing, seating nearly 4,000, the Bamboo Curtain, too, was rent.

Jian Qing, Mme Mao, inserted herself into the details, insisting on Beethoven's Fifth instead of the programmed Sixth. What was inadequate in the miscellany of parts cobbled together on site was provided from memory by the players. Between concerts Ormandy took a few minutes of a rehearsal with the nervous Central Philharmonic Orchestra of Beijing; the Philadelphia musicians watched tai-chi in the streets at dawn, played Frisbee with the locals, and gave impromptu music lessons.

In fact both the London Philharmonic and Vienna Philharmonic had just preceded Philadelphia in Beijing. But it was the American orchestra that made the news. Chinese musicians took courage: "Listening to classical music was a political activity at the time, it was so difficult to find. But then the orchestra came, and we felt as if spring were almost here."

Palestine and Israel

The Palestine Philharmonic, made up largely of European Jews in Eretz Israel, was a political act from the moment of its establishment in 1936 by the Polish violinist Bronisłav Hubermann. Toscanini's risky trip to conduct its inaugural performance was meant as a personal slap to Berlin. Thereafter, appearing in Israel became something of a rite of passage for politically engaged conductors. The very young Leonard Bernstein, seeking his fortune and his identity, appeared in Tel Aviv and Jerusalem on the heels of his first visit to Berlin. Charles Munch, an Alsatian Protestant raised in the orbit of Albert Schweitzer, came in 1947 and again later to inaugurate the Mann Auditorium in Tel Aviv. Zubin Mehta first appeared with the Israel Philharmonic in 1968 and became its first music director in 1977 and Music Director for Life in 1981.

In postwar Jerusalem, the music of Wagner was not tolerated. This long taboo was broken in July 2001 by Mehta's close friend Daniel Barenboim, appearing at the Israel Festival with his Berlin

Staatskapelle orchestra. The festival authorities had previously demanded a substitution for an excerpt from *Die Walküre*. Following the concert where Schumann and Stravinsky were played instead of Wagner, Barenboim turned to the audience to propose the *Tristan* prelude as an encore:

> Despite what the Israel Festival believes, there are people sitting in the audience for whom Wagner does not spark Nazi associations. I respect those for whom these associations are oppressive. It will be democratic to play a Wagner encore for those who wish to hear it. I am turning to you now and asking whether I can play Wagner.

A thirty-minute debate followed, with some audience members shouting "Fascist" at Barenboim and banging doors behind them as they walked out, but the great majority stayed. "If you're angry, be angry with me," Barenboim called, "but please don't be angry with the orchestra or the festival management." Barenboim was denounced by Israeli Prime Minister Ariel Sharon and President Moshe Katsav. The mayor of Jerusalem called the episode "brazen, arrogant, insensitive and uncivilized," and threatened to exclude Barenboim, an Israeli, from future appearances in the city.

In a much more substantial gesture than playing an encore, Barenboim in 1999, together with Edward Said, an outspoken Palestinian-American scholar on the faculty of Columbia University, founded what they called the West-Eastern Divan Orchestra. The reference is to Goethe's *West-östlicher Diwan*, twelve volumes of lyric poetry published in 1819 that celebrates encounters with the Orient. The orchestra, based in Seville, Spain, now includes young musicians from Israel, the Arab countries in the region, Iran and Turkey, and a few from Europe. Its charter calls for "mutual reflection" on the issues at hand. "We all know very well this is not going to solve the problems of the Middle East," Barenboim said. "Frankly, we are not interested in the political views of each and every one of the people that come and work with us, but the fact they come shows us that they are people who don't believe in a military solution to the conflict." On the occasion of the orchestra's appearance in Ramallah, on the West Bank, the *Jerusalem Post* wondered "With friends like Barenboim, who needs enemies?" "Why do we have to wait for the politicians," Barenboim insisted, "if we can do something now?"

10. The concertmaster of the West-Eastern Divan Orchestra warms up before a concert in Ramallah, 1999.

Pacifism and radical chic

Georg Solti, too, spoke and acted with forceful pacifist views. "All my life I have grown up in war and in revolution, both fascist and communist. It taught me passionately to believe in peace." Solti's World Orchestra for Peace was founded in 1995 on the occasion of the fiftieth anniversary of the United Nations, and continues to give a week of theme concerts every year or so. Yo-Yo Ma was a central figure in *Symphony 1997: Heaven, Earth, Mankind*, composed by Tan Dun on the occasion of the peaceful return of Hong Kong to China by the British. He also appeared with the Baghdad Philharmonic, aptly choosing the Fauré Elegy for Cello and Orchestra, at the Kennedy Center following the overthrow of Saddam Hussein. Noting President Bush and Secretary of State Colin Powell in the audience, the *Washington Post* headlined its coverage "The Sweet Sound of Propaganda." In 2006 the Baghdad orchestra numbered fewer than sixty musicians, rehearsing without electricity, short on materiel, in constant conflict with fundamentalists who allow no music at all. They make in the low hundreds of American dollars.

In 2008 the New York Philharmonic under Lorin Maazel visited North Korea, as closed a society as China had been in 1973. It was the largest group of outsiders ever let in at once: 400, including the 150 players and associates, eighty journalists, crews, and patrons who had each contributed $100,000 to underwrite the trip. The short visit—forty-eight hours in Pyongyang during the course of a much longer Asian tour—was nevertheless more immediate to observers than the Philadelphia in China, since it was live cast over the Internet with an audio feed to PBS. The audience consisted of 1,500 party members.

In many quarters the trip met with disapproval, since the New York Philharmonic could be read as catering elite entertainment to one of the cruelest governments on earth. Maazel spoke hopefully, and perhaps naively, of "opening a little door." The

White House press secretary sniped, "At the end of the day, we consider this concert to be a concert, and it's not a diplomatic coup," and the secretary of state, Condoleezza Rice (a formidable classical pianist), said, "I don't think we should get carried away with what listening to Dvořák is going to do in North Korea." Norman Lebrecht said the trip accomplished "precisely nothing." Undaunted, the New York Philharmonic went on to Hanoi in 2009, stopping in China on its way. Charles Rex, a violinist with the New York and formerly with the Philadelphia, had been on the tour of China and to Pyongyang. Rex marveled at changes he saw in the new China, thinking "we might have had a small role in helping a reclusive society open itself up."

The term "radical chic" was invented to describe Leonard Bernstein. Tom Wolfe's "That Party at Lenny's" was an irreverent look for *New York* magazine at a 1970 fund-raiser held in the Bernsteins' Park Avenue penthouse for the Black Panther Party. Few figures in orchestral history can have anguished so much as Bernstein did over personal identity and the place of one's music in the world at large. Raised in the heady liberalism of Harvard and Franklin Roosevelt, mentored by Copland and his progressive political and social views, he could not resist the notion of podium as pulpit. The Palestine Philharmonic had begged him to stay, in 1946, since he spoke Hebrew and was a Zionist at heart; in 1948 he led them for two months, thirty-five concerts, during the War of Independence. Later, in New York, he was devastated by the assassinations of the 1960s, and bitterly and sometimes incoherently opposed everything about the Ronald Reagan administration. He features in the Watergate tapes of September 1971, on the occasion of the *Mass* he had composed to a commission from Jacqueline Kennedy to inaugurate the Kennedy Center. President Nixon, tipped by his security apparatus as to the work's pacifist theme, skipped the premiere and in a follow-up discussion was told of Bernstein's weeping onstage after the performance and kissing everybody in sight, "including the big black guy" (Alvin Ailey, the choreographer). Nixon responded, "absolutely sickening."

At a commencement address at Johns Hopkins University in 1980, Bernstein challenged graduates to summon "the imaginative strength to liberate yourselves from the Cold War ambiance in which the eighties have already begun—along with all its accompanying paraphernalia of ever-proliferating borders, barriers, walls, passports, racial and sub-national fragmentation and re-fragmentation." He continued on this theme in an address prepared for Harvard in 1986, "Truth in a Time of War," for which his notes contain the bold scribble: "ENEMIES ARE OBSOLETE." Backing these theories with concrete action, he led the European Union Youth Orchestra on a 1985 Journey for Peace to Athens, Hiroshima, Budapest, and Vienna, symbolic places to reflect on the fortieth anniversary of the atomic bomb. In December 1989, Bernstein conducted the Berlin Celebration Concerts as the Berlin Wall was being dismantled, including a Christmas Day Beethoven's Ninth where the word "Freiheit" (freedom) was substituted for "Freude" (joy). The musicians came from both Germanys and the four occupying nations that had partitioned Berlin to begin with. This is only to touch on forty years of audacious gestures, not all of them so well reasoned but every one heartfelt.

The principal theme of Michael Steinberg's later writings— music as an agent of love—is implicitly pacifist. Music, "like any worthwhile partner in love, is demanding, sometimes exasperatingly, exhaustingly demanding," he wrote. "Its capacity to give is as near to infinite as anything in this world, and . . . what it offers us is always and inescapably in exact proportion to what we ourselves give." Asking his symphony audience to consider why we are here, he answered:

> We are here because of music. That music is a profession and
> a business cannot be written out of the world order, but let us
> remember in the midst of the swirl that it is also the subject of
> a contract full of words like attention, listening, meditation,
> reflection, remembrance, wit, joy, torment, delight, heart, brain,

spirit. Yes, the elevation of the spirit is the ultimate reward, the one that comes after we have learned to take that nourishment of the senses, the brain, and the heart. . . . The reason we are here is, as Friedrich Nietzsche said so simply, that "without music, life would be a mistake."

Conclusion: Civics

"The Orchestra Is Dead." Ernest Fleischmann, who did as much to keep the orchestra alive as anybody, was trying to drive home a point in so titling his 1987 commencement address to the graduates of the Cleveland Institute of Music. (Other uses of this rhetorical device include Pierre Boulez's call to "Burn Down All Opera Houses," and Milton Babbitt's "Who Cares If You Listen?"—*High Fidelity's* rather smart substitution for Babbitt's dryer original title.) "Long live the community of musicians," Fleischmann continued, then went on to daydream about a civic musical utopia where the orchestra is thoroughly woven into the fabric of everyday life. The model of two or three dozen weekends of subscription concerts yields nowadays to a catalog of offerings extending from chamber music and school visits to Facebook.

Joseph Horowitz fretted similarly about the corrective measures that needed taking for survival: recalibrating the monetary flow, de-glutting the pool of musicians and concerts, engaging the battle on multiple fronts. Reconceptualizing the symphony season, he thought, "may mean subscription concerts like Pacific Symphony's 'Tchaikovsky Portrait.' It may mean sending musicians to inner-city schools. It may mean collaborating with local museums and universities."

Proclamations of the death of culture, meanwhile, are not only tedious but also boring: "The Day the Music [the Movies, Democracy] Died," the vocabulary of morbidity and necromancy, amounts to fecklessness. Alex Ross protests the core formulation: that "classical music" has become coded as exclusive, exclusionary, irrelevant, and such alternatives as "art music" or "good/great music" carry much the same baggage in a world that measures its not inconsiderable musical appetite as songs in a playlist. Music is, after all, always dying, he notes.

Orchestras have a penchant for rebirth. Civic enterprise demands it. From Cleveland, where for all its problems the orchestra is typically described as "almost like church," came the idea of exporting the organization lock, stock, and barrel to the Sunbelt for an annual residency. (A Florida blogger characterized the repertoire of the first seasons as "Roasting Chestnuts.") For all the bad news, Detroit and Philadelphia seem likely to manage. The composer John Adams cautions that orchestra music and opera—the genres in which he himself excels—need not dominate music composition forever: in fact, they already don't. But the arrival of major new works in the symphony hall remains a reliable measure of civic life. "It has to do with the music you play, . . . with how you integrate yourself with the fabric of the community," Deborah Borda told an interviewer asking about the secret of her success.

The concert-finding website bachtrack.com lists in a given month some 500 orchestra concerts in 175 leading world venues. Fifty or more of these are in London, twenty-five or so in New York: in short, one or two major events each night. These figures may represent something of a decline from a halcyon symphonic past—calibrating the measure is no small task—but the offering is still robust.

Nor is it quite true about aging constituency, to judge from the numbers of young people involved in orchestral music. The European Union Youth Orchestra, established in 1978, consists of students fourteen to twenty-four years of age chosen from an annual audition pool of 4,000. Its founding conductor, Claudio Abbado, went on to establish Vienna's Gustav Mahler Jugendorchester in 1986, emphasizing opportunity for players from the Communist bloc countries. The new Los Angeles Youth Orchestra is meant to reach into the southern California megaregion as El Sistema did in impoverished Venezuela, where dozens of orchestras play to hundreds of thousands of listeners. Its centerpiece, the Simon Bolivar Youth Orchestra where Dudamel came to fame, plays Edinburgh and the Proms. Michael Tilson Thomas's New World Symphony Orchestra and YouTube Symphony Orchestra offer a current and fashionable line of products.

Young musicians in the first flush of discovering the great symphonic masterpieces afford us a powerful antidote to the tawdrier forms of pop culture and good grounds for optimism as to the future course of concert music. On Superbowl Sunday 2011 orchestra concerts were purposefully delayed to accommodate the football fans. Not much listenable music was to be heard from Dallas that afternoon—a flawed *Star-Spangled Banner* set amidst yards of billowing reds, whites, and blues, and uniforms as far as the eye could see; a halftime show that, to judge from Twitter, was hated by every living human being. (The dollar amounts were loathsome, too: $500 face value, $2,000 and up street value for the tickets; $3 million for a thirty-second commercial; $49 changing hands for every man, woman, and child in the country.) Less than an hour later, I was one of several hundred souls who came out for a program of the Brahms Double Concerto and Sibelius's Seventh, having paid $5 to $25 for the privilege. Nearly everyone there was hearing the Sibelius live for the first time. It was a college crowd, about half below the age of twenty-five and half above. At the close students gathered in one corner of the house for spirited Q&A; in the lobby well-wishers lingered nearly forty-five minutes and talked—knowledgeably—about the music they had heard. The campus provost, a Harvard/Oxford type who can recite conductor lineages and pinpoint the best recordings, was among the last to leave, apparently content. Nothing moribund there.

References

Chapter 1

Alan Rich, "Will Mehta Matter?" *New York*, August 28, 1978, 93.

Leonard Slatkin: press conference September 23, 2009, described in "Change Is in the Air," Detroit Symphony Orchestra weblog (blog. dso.org), September 24, 2009.

Charles Burney, *The Present State of Music in France and Italy: or, The Journal of a Tour Through Those Countries, Undertaken to Collect Materials for a General History of Music*, 2nd ed. (Oxford: T. Beckett, 1773), 336.

Charles de Brosses, writing from Venice to M. de Blancey in August 1739, widely quoted in English beginning with Marc Pincherle, *Vivaldi: Genius of the Baroque* (New York: W. W. Norton, 1957), 19.

Dr. Burney on Pagin: Burney, 44.

"Soberly, modestly, quietly." Contract between Prince Nikolaus Esterházy and the flutist Franz Sigl, April 1781, cited by H. C. Robbins Landon, "Haydn and Eighteenth-Century Patronage," Tanner Lectures on Human Values, Clare Hall, Cambridge University, February 25–26, 1983 (www.tannerlectures.utah. edu), 161.

On the Mannheim Orchestra: Christian Friedrich Schubart, writing in about 1780 (*Ideen zu einer Aesthetik der Tonkunst*), quoted by Richard Taruskin in *Music in the Seventeenth and Eighteenth Centuries* (New York: Oxford University Press, 2009), 506.

"I am Salomon from London." Recounted by Albert Christoph Dies in his biography of Haydn (1810), quoted by Jens Peter Larsen, *Haydn* (New York: W. W. Norton, 1997), 59.

Haydn's appearance in London: Burney, describing Haydn's concert of March 11, 1791; "Sixteen Concerts in a Week," both quoted by Simon McVeigh, *Concert Life in London from Mozart to Haydn* (Cambridge: Cambridge University Press, 2006), 1–2.

Coachmen and their horses: [London] Philharmonic Society program, May 1, 1826.

Beethoven's genius: Prince Nicolas Galitzin to Beethoven, April 8, 1824, praising the *Missa solemnis*, quoted by Beethoven's secretary Anton Schindler in *Beethoven As I Knew Him*, ed. Donald W. MacArdle (1966; rpt. New York: Dover, 1996), 302.

Higginson to Boston Symphony orchestra manager Charles Ellis, (1905), quoted by Joseph Horowitz in *Classical Music in America: A History of Its Rise and Fall* (New York: W. W. Norton, 2005), 76.

Virgil Thomson, "Bigger Than Baseball," *New York Herald Tribune*, 1953, in *Virgil Thomson: A Reader: Selected Writings, 1924–1984*, ed. Richard Kostelanetz (New York: Routledge, 2002), 61–64.

Chapter 2

Society of British and Foreign Musicians described by George Grove in the first and subsequent editions of his *Dictionary of Music and Musicians*, vol. 4 (London, 1890), 544.

On Doriot Anthony Dwyer: "Boston Picks a Woman," *Time* magazine, October 13, 1952; *Springfield Morning Union*, October 20, 1952; *Boston Globe*, October 12, 1952.

On Orin O'Brien: "Orchestras: Ladies' Day," *Time*, December 9, 1966.

"Musical Misogyny (*Musikalische Misogynie*): An Interview of the Vienna Philharmonic by the West German State Radio," February 13, 1996, a transcription and translation of the broadcast by William Osborne, osborne-conant.org, quoting Roland Girtler, Viennese sociologist; Dieter Flury, flute; and Helmut Zehetner, violin.

"After 70 Years, Philadelphia Symphony Hires First Blacks," *Jet*, October 29, 1970.

Mike Lewin, "All Recording Stops Today / Disc Firms Sit Back, Public's Next Move / Government May Step In; Threat of CIO Seen; Several Months' Record Supply on Hand," *DownBeat* 9/15 (August 1, 1942).

David Frum, "Detroit's Symphony Goes with Big Labor," frumforum. com, February 19, 2011.

International Conference of Symphony and Opera Musicians, "Charlotte Ratifies 4-Year Modified and Extended Agreement," settlement bulletin, November 30, 2009.

Michael H. Hodges, "DSO Patrons, Politicians Disappointed by Season Cancellation / Negotiations are Over," *Detroit News*, February 20, 2011, quoting Maria Eliason ("a piano teacher in Grosse Pointe Park and season ticket holder for 15 years").

Andrew Stewart, "Brazilian Orchestra in Bitter Jobs Dispute," *Classical Music*, April 5, 2011.

Hilary Burrage, "Orchestral Salaries in the UK," *Dreaming Realist* weblog (dreamingrealist.co.uk), November 5, 2007.

Kim Ode, "Shadows & Light," interview of Jorja Fleezanis and Michael Steinberg, *Minneapolis StarTribune*, June 12, 2009.

Chapter 3

Andrew Carnegie, address May 13, 1890, quoted in *Carnegie Hall Then and Now*, brochure (New York: Carnegie Hall Archives, 2010), 1.

Leo Beranek, *Riding the Waves: A Life in Sound, Science, and Industry* (Cambridge, MA: MIT Press, 2008), x.

Marin Alsop, quoted in Tom Manoff, "Do Electronics Have a Place in the Concert Hall? Maybe," *New York Times*, March 31, 1991.

David Ng, "Frank Gehry Remembers L. A. Philharmonic's Ernest Fleischmann," *Los Angeles Times*, June 14, 2010.

Ernest Fleischmann, "Who Runs Our Orchestras and Who Should?" *High Fidelity / Musical America* 19/1 (January 1969):59.

Mark Swed, "The 'Rite' Springs to Life Under Salonen's Baton: An Electric Performance by the Los Angeles Philharmonic and Its Director Is Rapturously Received in Paris," *Los Angeles Times*, October 3, 1996; cited by James S. Russell in "Project Diary: The Story of How Frank Gehry's Design and Lillian Disney's Dream Were Ultimately Rescued to Create the Masterful Walt Disney Concert Hall," *Architectural Record* 191/11 (November 2003): 135–51.

Chapter 4

Samuel Rosenbaum quotation and "They create money where none exists," Helen M. Thompson, *Handbook for Symphony Orchestra Women's Associations* (Vienna, VA: American Symphony Orchestra League, 1963), 5.

"Chain-Store Music," *Time*, February 6, 1939.

"The Ford Foundation: Millions for Music—Music for Millions," *Music Educators Journal* 53/1 (September 1956): 83–86 (84).

"Elephant Task Force." Andrew W. Mellon Foundation Orchestra Forum, *A Journey Toward New Visions for Orchestras, 2003–2008: A Report by the Elephant Task Force*, April 2008.

Deborah Borda, "Drawn to the Music," *New York Times*, April 10, 2010.

The Wolf Organization, Inc., *The Financial Condition of Symphony Orchestras, part I: The Orchestra Industry, June 1992* (Washington, DC: American Symphony Orchestra League, 1992), with responses included in the appendix. Peter Pastreich's response constitutes Appendix D.

Chapter 5

Hector Berlioz, letter to Théodore Ritter, [July 4], 1855, in *Correspondance générale* V, ed. Hugh J. Macdonald and François Lesure (Paris: Flammarion, 1989), 124.

Mendelssohn as remembered by Eduard Devrient, in *My Recollections of Felix Mendelssohn-Bartholdy, and His Letters to Me*, trans. Natalia MacFarren (London: Richard Bentley, 1869), 60.

Leopold Stokowski, in an anecdote widely, and variously, recounted, including by Jeremy Siepmann, "The History of Direction and Conducting," in *The Cambridge Companion to the Orchestra*, ed. Colin Lawson (Cambridge: Cambridge University Press, 2003), 124.

Thomas Beecham, in Eileen Miller, *The Edinburgh International Festival, 1947–1996* (Aldershot, Hants.: Ashgate, 1996), 19.

"Now we can play without ulcers." G. Y. Loveridge, "Munch, New Conductor, Brings Joy to the Boston Symphony," *Providence Sunday Journal*, January 29, 1950.

Alex Ross, "The Anti-Maestro: Esa-Pekka Salonen at the Los Angeles Philharmonic," *Listen to This* (New York: Farrar, Straus and Giroux, 2010), 103.

Chapter 6

"Lasting value, links to tradition, individuality, and familiarity." Peter Burkholder, "The Twentieth Century and the Orchestra as Museum," in *The Orchestra: Origins and Transformations*, ed. Joan Peyser (New York: Scribner's, 1986; rpt. Milwaukee: Hal Leonard, 2006), 413.

"Louvre of Music." Antoine Elwart, *Histoire de la Société des Concerts du Conservatoire Impérial de Musique* (Paris: Castel, 1860), 287.

Lawrence Kramer, *Why Classical Music Still Matters* (Berkeley: University of California Press, 2007), 12.

Chapter 7

Berlioz on Beethoven's "Eroica" Symphony (*Revue et Gazette musicale*, April 9, 1837), trans. mine, but see also *Hector Berlioz, A Critical Study of Beethoven's Nine Symphonies* (1913; rpt. Urbana: University of Illinois Press, 2000), 44.

Schumann on Berlioz's *Fantastique: Neue Zeitschrift für Musik* 3 (1835), in installments July 3–August 14, best trans. as "Robert Schumann: A Symphony by Berlioz," in *Hector Berlioz, Fantastic Symphony: An Authoritative Score, Historical Background, Analysis, Views and Comments*, ed. Edward T. Cone (New York: W. W. Norton, 1971), 220–48. On Brahms: "Neue Bahnen," *NzfM* 39/18 (October 28, 1853), trans. in *Robert Schumann, On Music and Musicians*, ed. Konrad Wolff, trans. Paul Rosenfeld (New York: Pantheon, 1946), 253–54.

Debussy, "Impressions of the *Ring* in London," *Gil Blas*, June 1, 1903, as trans. in *Debussy on Music*, ed. François Lesure, trans. Richard Langham Smith (Ithaca, NY: Cornell University Press, 1977), 203.

Virgil Thomson, "Conservative Institution" (*New York Herald Tribune*, 1947), in *Virgil Thomson, A Reader: Selected Writings, 1924–1984*, ed. Richard Kostelanetz (New York: Routledge, 2002), 57.

David Cairns, "Karajan the Conqueror" (*London Sunday Times*, 1958), in *Responses* (1973; rpt. New York: Da Capo, 1980), 165.

Virgil Thomson, "The Appreciation-racket," subchapter of "Why Composers Write How" (*New York Herald Tribune*, 1939, rev. 1962), in *Virgil Thomson: A Reader*, 32.

Theodor W. Adorno, "Analytical Study of the *NBC Music Appreciation Hour*," *Musical Quarterly* 78 (1994): 327.

Richard Taruskin, "Resisting the Ninth," in *Text and Act: Essays on Music and Performance* (New York: Oxford University Press, 1995), 245.

Michael Steinberg, "Why We Are Here," in *For the Love of Music: Invitations to Listening*, with Larry Rothe (New York: Oxford University Press, 2006), 238.

Michael Steinberg, "Bernstein's 'Kaddish' in Premiere Here," *Boston Globe*, February 1, 1964.

Robert Spano to the *Atlanta Journal-Constitution*, May 21, 2007; quoted by Henry Fogel, "Trouble in Atlanta: The *Atlanta*

Journal-Constitution Situation," *On the Record/ArtsJournal* weblog (artsjournal.com/ontherecord), May 30, 2007.

Alan Rich to Laura Stegman, April 8, 2008, as reported by Kevin Roderick, "Alan Rich Out as Weekly Critic," *LA Observed* weblog (laobserved.com), April 9, 2008.

Daniel J. Wakin, "Newspapers Trimming Classical Critics," *New York Times*, June 9, 2007.

Susan McClary, "Getting Down Off the Beanstalk," *Minnesota Composers Forum Newsletter*, January 1987; considerably softened in *Feminine Endings* (Minneapolis: University of Minnesota Press, 1991), 128.

Alan Rich, "Gustav, Gustavo, Buon Gusto," *So I've Heard* weblog (soiveheard.com), October 23, 2009.

Box 7.1 New York *Musical Courier*, November 9, 1904, in Nicolas Slonimsky, *Lexicon of Musical Invective: Critical Assaults on Composers Since Beethoven's Time* (1953, rpt. New York: W. W. Norton, 2000), 120.

Chapter 8

"Here, finally, was real music." Piero Coppola, *Dix-sept ans de musique à Paris, 1922–39* (Lausanne: F. Rouge & Cie, 1944; rpt. Paris: Slatkine, 1982), 60.

Walter Legge quoted by Norman Lebrecht, *Who Killed Classical Music?: Maestros, Managers, and Corporate Politics* (Secaucus, NJ: Carol Publishing, 1997), 303.

Boston Symphony Orchestra concert programs, January 1935, in James H. North, *Boston Symphony Orchestra: An Augmented Discography* (New York: Scarecrow, 2008), 8.

"Another Beethoven cycle." Lebrecht, *Who Killed Classical Music?*, 317.

Chapter 9

Richard Strauss on Mahler, marginalia in a copy of Alma Mahler's memoirs (1940); quoted by Henry-Louis de La Grange, *Gustav Mahler: Vienna: Triumph and Disillusion (1904–1907)* (Oxford: Oxford University Press, 1995), 198.

"I have never before heard Beethoven's Ninth like that." Gustav Altmann in the *Strassburger Post*, May 27, 1911; quoted by La Grange, *Mahler: Triumph and Disillusion*, 202.

"Weapons stayed in their cases." *Le Courrier musical*, April 1917, 209.

Dwight D. Eisenhower, letter to Henry B. Cabot (chairman, Boston Symphony Orchestra), September 28, 1956; pub. in "Eisenhower Lauds Boston Symphony," *New York Times*, October 6, 1956.

"We couldn't spend it all." Frances Stonor Saunders, *Who Paid the Piper? The CIA and the Cultural Cold War* (London: Granta, 1999), 105; her source was Gilbert Greenway.

Xiyun Yang, "U.S. Orchestra Performs in China, in Echoes of 1973," *New York Times*, May 7, 2010.

Daniel Barenboim and Wagner in Israel: "Despite what the Israel Festival believes," quoted by Ewen MacAskill (in Jerusalem), "Barenboim Stirs up Israeli Storm by Playing Wagner," *Guardian*, July 9, 2001. Other quotes in Joel Greenberg, "Playing a Bit of Wagner Sets Off an Uproar in Israel," *New York Times*, July 9, 2001. "We all know very well this is not going to solve the problems of the Middle East," in "As the Cycle of Violence Escalates, Barenboim Takes His Arab-Israeli Orchestra to Play for Peace," *Independent*, August 22, 2003.

Georg Solti, interview Geneva 1995 at a concert of the World Orchestra for Peace, worldorchestraforpeace.com (with video).

Philadelphia Orchestra in Pyongyang. "Opening a little door"; Dvořák in North Korea: quoted by Thomas Omestad, "The New York Philharmonic Tries to Strike the Right Notes in North Korea," *U.S. News & World Report*, February 26, 2008. "Not a diplomatic coup": Dana Perino (White House press secretary), quoted by Daniel J. Wakin, "North Koreans Welcome Symphonic Diplomacy," *New York Times*, February 27, 2008. Norman Lebrecht, "Some Good News Comes from the New York Philharmonic," *Slipped Disc/ArtsJournal* weblog (artsjournal.com/slippeddisc), January 12, 2009.

Charles Rex, "Musings on the New York Philharmonic's North Korean Concert," polyphonic.org, March 20, 2008.

Alex Ross, "Bernstein in the Nixon Tapes," *New Yorker*, August 11, 2009. Leonard Bernstein, "Commencement Speech at Johns Hopkins," May 30, 1980, at leonardbernstein.com; "Truth in a Time of War" (1986) introduced by Carol J. Oja and Mark Eden Orowitz ("Something Called Terrorism"), *American Scholar* 77/4 (September 2008): 71–79.

"Musical heaven is attainable." Steinberg, "Why We Are Here," 242.

Conclusion

Ernest Fleischmann, "The Orchestra Is Dead; Long Live the Community of Musicians," address given at the commencement exercises of the Cleveland Institute of Music, May 16, 1987.

Joseph Horowitz, "Looking Beyond the Cleveland Strike," *The Unanswered Question/ArtsJournal* weblog (artsjournal.com/uq), January 23, 2010.

Deborah Borda, quoted by Daniel J. Wakin, "Philharmonic President Is to Depart, as Music World Changes," *New York Times*, September 27, 2010.

Further reading

General works on the orchestra

Carse, Adam. *The Orchestra from Beethoven to Berlioz: A History of the Orchestra in the First Half of the Nineteenth Century*. Cambridge: Heffer & Sons, 1948.

Carse, Adam. *The Orchestra in the Eighteenth Century*. Cambridge: Heffer & Sons, 1940.

Lawson, Colin, ed. *The Cambridge Companion to the Orchestra*. Cambridge: Cambridge University Press, 2003.

Peyser, Joan, ed. *The Orchestra: Origins and Transformations*. New York: Scribners, 1986 (rpt. as *The Orchestra: A Collection of 23 Essays on Its Origins and Transformations*, Milwaukee, WI: Hal Leonard, 2006).

Spitzer, John, and Neal Zaslaw. *The Birth of the Orchestra: History of an Institution, 1650–1815*. New York: Oxford University Press, 2004.

Spitzer, John, and Neal Zaslaw. "Orchestra," in *Grove Music Online* (*oxfordmusiconline.com*).

Orchestras and philharmonic societies

Ardoin, John. *The Philadelphia Orchestra: A Century of Music*. Philadelphia: Temple University Press, 1999.

Cooper, Jeffrey. *The Rise of Instrumental Music and Concert Series in Paris: 1828–1871*. Ann Arbor, MI: UMI Research Press, 1983.

Ehrlich, Cyril. *First Philharmonic: A History of the Royal Philharmonic Society*. Oxford: Clarendon Press, 1995.

Hart, Philip. *Orpheus in the New World: The Symphony Orchestra as an American Cultural Institution*. New York: W. W. Norton, 1973.

Holoman, D. Kern. *The Société des Concerts du Conservatoire, 1828–1967*. Berkeley: University of California Press, 2004.

Horowitz, Joseph. *Classical Music in America: A History of Its Rise and Fall*. New York: W. W. Norton, 2005.

Koury, Daniel J. *Orchestral Performance Practices in the Nineteenth Century: Size, Proportions, and Seating*. Ann Arbor, MI: UMI Research Press, 1986.

Levine, Lawrence W. *Highbrow/Lowbrow: The Emergence of Cultural Hierarchy in America*. Cambridge, MA: Harvard University Press, 1988.

McVeigh, Simon. *Concert Life in London from Mozart to Haydn*. Cambridge: Cambridge University Press, 2006.

Rosenberg, Donald. *The Cleveland Orchestra Story: "Second to None."* Cleveland: Gray & Company, 2000.

Rothe, Larry. *Music for a City, Music for the World: 100 Years with the San Francisco Symphony*. San Francisco: Chronicle Books, 2011.

Shanet, Howard. *Philharmonic: A History of New York's Orchestra*. New York: Doubleday, 1975.

Stewart, Andrew. *The LSO at 90: From Queen's Hall to the Barbican Centre*. London: London Symphony Orchestra, 1994.

Labor and management

Ayer, Julie. *More Than Meets the Ear: How Symphony Musicians Made Labor History*. Minneapolis, MN: Syren Book Co., 2005.

Seltzer, George. *Music Matters: The Performer and the American Federation of Musicians*. Metuchen, NJ: Scarecrow, 1989.

Venues

Beranek, Leo. *Concert Halls and Opera Houses: Music, Acoustics, and Architecture*. 2nd ed. New York: Springer Verlag, 2004.

Beranek, Leo. *Riding the Waves: A Life in Sound, Science, and Industry*. Cambridge, MA: MIT Press, 2008.

Jaffe, Lee, J. Christopher Jaffe, and Leo L. Beranek. *The Acoustics of Performance Halls: Spaces for Music from Carnegie Hall to the Hollywood Bowl*. New York: W. W. Norton, 2010.

Thompson, Emily. *The Soundscape of Modernity: Architectural Acoustics and the Culture of Listening in America, 1900–1933*. Cambridge, MA: MIT Press, 2002.

Money

Baumol, William J., and William G. Bowen. *Performing Arts: The Economic Dilemma; A Study of Problems Common to Theater, Opera, Music, and Dance*. New York: Twentieth Century Fund, 1966.

Lebrecht, Norman. *Who Killed Classical Music?: Maestros, Managers, and Corporate Politics*. Secaucus, NJ: Carol Publishing, 1997.

Conducting and conductors

The Art of Conducting: Great Conductors of the Past. Hamburg: Teldec Video, 1994.

Bamberger, Carl. *The Conductor's Art*. New York: Columbia University Press, 1965.

Bowen, José, ed. *The Cambridge Companion to Conducting*. Cambridge: Cambridge University Press, 2003.

Charry, Michael. *George Szell: A Life of Music*. Urbana: University of Illinois Press, 2011.

Galkin, Elliott W. *A History of Orchestral Conducting in Theory and Practice*. Stuyvesant, NY: Pendragon, 1988.

Heyworth, Peter. *Otto Klemperer: His Life and Times*. 2 vols. Cambridge: Cambridge University Press, 1983–1996.

Holden, Raymond. *The Virtuoso Conductors: The Central European Tradition from Wagner to Karajan*. New Haven, CT: Yale University Press, 2005.

Holoman, D. Kern. *Charles Munch*. New York: Oxford University Press, 2012.

Horowitz, Joseph. *Understanding Toscanini: A Social History of American Concert Life*. Berkeley: University of California Press, 1994.

Kenyon, Nicholas. *Simon Rattle: From Birmingham to Berlin*. Rev. ed. London: Faber & Faber, 2001.

Lebrecht, Norman. *The Maestro Myth: Great Conductors in Pursuit of Power*. London: Simon & Schuster, 1991.

Repertoire

Kramer, Lawrence. *Why Classical Music Still Matters*. Berkeley: University of California Press, 2009.

Lawson, Colin, and Robin Stowell. *The Historical Performance of Music: An Introduction*. Cambridge: Cambridge University Press, 1999.

Ross, Alex. *Listen to This*. New York: Farrar, Straus & Giroux, 2010.

Ross, Alex. *The Rest Is Noise: Listening to the Twentieth Century*. New York: Farrar, Straus & Giroux, 2007.

Taruskin, Richard. *Text and Act: Essays on Music and Performance*. New York: Oxford University Press, 1995.

Weber, William. *Music and the Middle Class: The Social Structure of Concert Life in London, Paris, and Vienna Between 1830 and 1848*. Aldershot, Hants: Ashgate, 2004.

Program notes

Steinberg, Michael. *Choral Masterworks: A Listener's Guide*. New York: Oxford University Press, 2005.

Steinberg, Michael. *The Concerto: A Listener's Guide*. New York: Oxford University Press, 1998.

Steinberg, Michael. *The Symphony: A Listener's Guide*. New York: Oxford University Press, 1995.

Tovey, Donald Francis. *Essays in Musical Analysis*. London: Oxford University Press, 1935–1939.

Criticism

Cairns, David. *Responses: Musical Essays and Reviews*. Rev. ed. New York: Da Capo, 1980.

Debussy, Claude. *Debussy on Music: The Critical Writings of the Great French Composer Claude Debussy*. Edited by François Lesure. Translated by Richard Langham Smith. New York: Knopf, 1977.

Hanslick, Eduard. *Hanslick's Music Criticisms*. Edited by Henry Pleasants. New York: Dover, 1988.

Schumann, Robert. *Schumann on Music: A Selection from the Writings*. Edited by Henry Pleasants. Annotated ed. New York: Dover, 1988.

Thomson, Virgil. *Virgil Thomson: A Reader: Selected Writings, 1924–1984*. Edited by Richard Kostelanetz. New York: Routledge, 2002.

Recordings

Lebrecht, Norman. *Maestros, Masterpieces, and Madness: The Secret Life and Shameful Death of the Classical Record Industry*. London: Allen Lane, 2007. Published in the United States as *The Life and Death of Classical Music: Featuring the 100 Best and 20 Worst Recordings Ever Made*. New York: Anchor, 2007.

Orchestras and politics

Kraus, Richard Curt. *Pianos and Politics in China: Middle-Class Ambitions and the Struggle over Western Music.* New York: Oxford University Press, 1989.

Saunders, Frances Stonor. *The Cultural Cold War: The CIA and the World of Arts and Letters.* New York: New Press, 2000.

Seldes, Barry. *Leonard Bernstein: The Political Life of an American Musician.* Berkeley: University of California Press, 2009.

Steinberg, Michael, and Larry Rothe. *For the Love of Music: Invitations to Listening.* New York: Oxford University Press, 2006.

Taubman, Howard. *The Symphony Orchestra Abroad.* Vienna, VA: American Symphony Orchestra League, 1970.

Index

Index